TENNIS MADE EASY

DYNAMIC CPR SYSTEM

FOR TEACHING AND PLAYING

YOGA
OF MIND AND BODY

FOR TENNIS AND OTHER SPORTS

AND FOR FITNESS

INCLUDES MIND MANAGEMENT

Dr. Rajah Sekaran

First edition published in 2017
Second edition published in 2018
M. Rajah Sekaran, Member, Yogesha, LLC
Email: mrajsekar@yahoo.com

First edition published in 2017
Second edition published in 2018
M. Rajah Sekaran, Member, Yogesha, LLC
Email: mrajsekar@yahoo.com

First edition published in 2017
Second edition published in 2018
M. Rajah Sekaran, Member, Yogesha, LLC
Email: mrajsekar@yahoo.com

© M. Rajah Sekaran 2017
All rights reserved. This book is protected under the copyright laws of the United States of America and other countries. Except for reviews and quotations, use or republication of any part of this work is prohibited, without prior written permission from the author who holds the copyright.

ISBN # 978-1973744733

International ISBN # 1973744732

Library of Congress Copyright Office in accordance with

    Title 17, *United States Code,*

    Registration Number TXu 2-015-529

Library of Congress Control #2017913797

Create space Independent Publishing Platform

North Charleston, SC

I LEARNED THIS AT LEAST, BY MY EXPERIMENT:
THAT IF ONE ADVANCES CONFIDENTLY IN THE DIRECTION OF HIS DREAMS AND ENDEAVORS TO LIVE THE LIFE WHICH HE HAS IMAGINED HE WILL MEET WITH A SUCCESS UNEXPECTED IN COMMON HOURS.
    HENRY DAVID THOREAU
    (1817–1863)

TABLE OF CONTENTS

1. TENNIS– THE DYNAMIC CPR SYSTEM OF CONSTANT POINTS OF REFERENCE…pg. 1

2. THE GRIP………………………………….. pg. 49

3. YOGA APPLICATIONS FOR SPORTS AND FITNESS – BODY MECHANICS… pg. 53

4. MIND MECHANICS……………………… pg. 134

5. MIND MANAGEMENT……………………. pg. 148

6. PRANAYAMA………………………….pg. 161

7. ON MEDITATION…………………………....…….pg. 176

PLEASE NOTE

M. Rajah Sekaran, Member, Yogesha LLC, the author and publisher, and Vasanthi Bhat, the yoga teacher who provided her yoga photos from VasanthaYoga, disclaim any implied warranty, guarantee, liability, loss or injury in connection with any of the information or suggestion, described in this book.

The author and publisher are not engaged in rendering medical or any other kind of personal, professional services in this book. You are advised to consult appropriate medical or professional help for all matters related to health, before using the information and suggestions given in this book.

Dedicated to *All my Teachers*

Lynne Rolley

My Tennis Guru

Executive Director of Tennis
La Quinta a Waldorf Astoria Resort and Club
Palm Springs, California

Previous Director of Women's Tennis for the USTA,
Coaching Jennifer Capriatti and
U.S. Open Winner Lindsey Davenport

Previous Director of Tennis at The Berkeley Tennis Club, Berkeley, California

The first woman to coach a men's collegiate tennis team in the United States.

The author, Dr. Rajah Sekaran is a retired physician living in California with his wife. They have three grown children.

The author used his knowledge of human anatomy from his medical education, and experimenting with the ball machine for hundreds of hours, came up with his focus based system of playing and teaching Tennis. The system is called Dynamic CPR System which stands for Constant Point of Reference, explaining what to focus on, and how to focus in the game of Tennis. The author's father introduced him to tennis and yoga in his teenage years, and is uniquely qualified in combining both. Regarding yoga, he taught Hatha Yoga, Pranayama, and Meditation both with his father and independently for many years.

ACKNOWLEDGEMENTS

This is the essence of all I have learned over the years in both Yoga and Tennis from many, many teachers. I am very thankful to all my teachers, including my father who introduced me to Tennis as well as Yoga in my teenage years.

In the recent past years, Lynne Rolley has been my tennis Guru at Berkeley Tennis Club. Lynne Rolley was the Director of Tennis in Berkeley Tennis Club for many years and currently, is the Executive Director of Tennis at La Quinta Resort and Club (a Waldorf Astoria Resort) in Palm Springs, California; and well known as having coached US Open winner Lindsey Davenport and Jennifer Capriati. I am grateful to Lynne for having introduced me to the focus-based playing of tennis.

Before that, I have also had lessons from Wendel Pierce, the Pro at Chabot Racquet Club. I am thankful to Wendel for teaching me the fundamentals of Tennis playing.

In yoga, I have had different teachers for the various disciplines of yoga, which I found them to be different pieces of a puzzle. At some point the pieces come together to reveal the ultimate goal of yoga. So I am grateful to all my teachers. Particularly, I am thankful to my father for teaching me *Hatha Yoga, Pranayama and Meditation.* I learned the *Gnana Yoga, the Yoga of wisdom* from Swami Dayananda Saraswati and Swami Shraddhananda by attending their numerous lectures and camps; and also direct one-on-one instruction and *initiation.* I am very grateful to both of them.

I am grateful to Vasanthi Bhat, a Yoga teacher. Vasanthi acknowledges Swami Satyananda Saraswati, a disciple of Swami Sivananda, as her yoga guru. 32 of the Yoga photographs in the chapter on Yoga in this book were provided by Vasanthi Bhat, founder, director of Vasantha Yoga, San Jose, California (www.vasanthayoga.com). Used with permission. I am also thankful to Mahabaleshwar K.P. Bhat for editing and preparing the CD of the Yoga photographs from Vasanthi.

My father originally learned yoga when he was in college from Swami Sivananda and much later from his disciple, Swami Vishnu Devananda. I learned from my father, and also from the disciples of Swami Sivananda. Essentially, Vasanthi Bhat and I both follow the teaching methods of Swami Sivananda. So, I found it appropriate to use photographs of Vasanthi Bhat in the Yoga section of this book.

Jeff Robinson is a world traveler and professional photographer of unusual birds, animals and people from all over the globe. I am extremely thankful to Jeff for taking the high-quality photographs of me for this book.

Alan Freeland is a Patent Attorney practicing in San Francisco, and a member of The Berkeley Tennis Club, Berkeley, California. We have had insightful discussions on different topics from mind to mysticism over a cup of coffee at The Berkeley Tennis Club many times, and we continue our sessions. I am very thankful to Alan for the stimulating conversations and especially for helping me with his legal expertise for this book.

I am very thankful to Sunaina Sekaran for editing the final manuscript, typing the text as needed, and arranging the photographs. I am amazed at the knowledge and quickness that my granddaughter possesses at her young age.

My daughter Shanthi Sekaran PhD, a fiction writer, teaches Creative Writing at the college level and has published two novels. Shanthi is my *writing guru* who taught me the fundamentals of *writing*. She also edited most of the text of this book; I am very thankful to Shanthi.

I am also grateful to Spencer Dutton, Shanthi's husband for correcting many of the computer glitches, during my writing in the past four years. It goes without saying, it took me longer than four years to write this book.

I am especially thankful to my wife, Surabhi Sekaran, M.D, for letting me take away the family time to write in those years.

INTRODUCTION

I started learning yoga and tennis in my teen-years; and I continue to be a student of both.

Both are like the ocean; if tennis is the Atlantic Ocean, yoga is the Pacific. In that sense, they do intermingle with each other. In Mind management, I use the yoga of wisdom or Gnana yoga. In the Body mechanics, I emphasize the importance of daily routine of *asanas* from the discipline of Hatha yoga; and in selecting the yoga exercises, I have paid particular attention to yoga postures that will help general fitness as well as any sports activity, especially, the game of tennis; and in preventing injuries.

I feel strongly that just stretching for a few minutes before the game is helpful but not enough. Daily yoga-practice with the recommended postures will help to keep the joints supple and flexible and the body and mind healthy.

There are hundreds of books on tennis and yoga with a comprehensive description of all available techniques. Besides there is a wealth of *encyclopedic* style of information in the Internet on the same subjects. So, I did not want to add one more book in the same approach. Herein I have focused only on the techniques that has been proven by personal experience to be beneficial and practical in the game of tennis for all levels, reinforced by yoga postures for the body, mind and the breathing. For example, in preparing for a tennis match, push-ups may strain the shoulders, especially before the match; and so they are replaced by a different set of core-exercises.

CPR stands for *Constant Point of Reference*. This is a *focus based technique* for a *natural way* of playing tennis and the movements are graceful, effective and less prone to injuries. This dynamic system of reference points was compiled by the author, after playing tennis for many years and after hundreds of hours of experimenting with the tennis ball-machine, at various speed and spin levels at varying frequencies; and after serving thousands of practice-serves. The details of the CPR system are explained in the following pages. Teaching my grandchildren was also helpful in developing this system.

Using the CPR system, the player *focuses* on a single point— the Reference Point— at the moment of truth, on executing the shot or serve. Any planning or placement of the ball at a certain location has to occur before the player commits his focus on the Reference Point. Focusing on the placement or the opponent at the time of hitting will not help; it will only hinder his focus on the ball.

IMPORTANCE OF DRILLS

This CPR system does not mean that body movement drills are not important. It is essential to do such drills to learn, for example, to move forwards for an approach shot or volley, and to move back and sideways for an overhead shot. This is further explained in the text on the 'Dynamic CPR system'

HOW THE CPR SYSTEM WORKS:
This is a *focus based natural approach* to body movement and execution of shots and serves. *Focusing* on each of the corresponding reference points, helps the player to *command* the body and mind:

1. to arrive at the right position at the right moment
2. to move the body to execute the appropriate shot or serve
3. to maintain balance before, during and after the shot or serve and
4. to maintain focus before, during and after the shot.

For example, when we throw a frisbee in front of a *retriever*, it runs, jumps and catches the edge of the frisbee precisely, with its teeth. Nobody taught the dog how to run to the frisbee, when to take long strides or when to take short shuffles, in order to catch it. The retriever *focused* on the edge of the frisbee as its *reference point* and coordinated its body and mind:

1. to arrive at the right location and

2. to catch the frisbee with balance, focus and grace, and got the reward of a biscuit for doing it!

It is almost impossible to learn specific bodily movements and racquet positions for all different game situations. There are just too many variables for 1.the ball and the racquet position, 2.the player's position, flexibility and conditioning, and 3.the opponent's actions and reactions, and finally 4.the weather; yes, even the weather variations can affect a game.

I happened to spend a few weeks in Nottingham, England in the middle of winter; I arranged to play at the local tennis club daily during my stay. Nottingham is in the Midlands region of England. It drizzles very frequently and sometimes the drizzle becomes rain, especially in the winter. So, there is always some moisture in the air; the courts and the balls can become slightly wet but still playable. My tennis colleagues in Nottingham advised me to hit the ball *harder* than usual, by swinging the racquet faster; so, hitting with pace became a habit for me. When I came back home to California, my friends were wondering how my shots were coming back at a higher speed than before. When you try hitting slightly moist balls, you can appreciate the difference moisture and humidity can make in hitting the ball.

Similarly, the *wind* also can be a variable factor in the game of tennis. For example, when the wind is blowing against the direction of the player, the serving may require a higher speed than usual or a kick-serve may be appropriate. If the wind is blowing in the direction of the play, it is advisable for the server to stand two or three inches behind the baseline to compensate the wind-factor, while serving. Alternately, serving with a *spin* will keep the ball inside the service-box. The same is true for forehand shots and backhand shots.

The CPR system can lessen the effects of variables, mentioned above; and help the players of all levels and all ages to teach and play a better game of tennis.

THE PURPOSE
1) TO PROMOTE TENNIS
Using this *Dynamic CPR System* of playing tennis,

tennis mom or any parent, for example, who plays tennis at a reasonable level will be able to teach his or her children to learn and improve the game of tennis, further reinforcing what the player learns in the tennis clinics and lessons.

This technique of *focus-based natural* way of playing tennis can help the player at any level to improve the game to the next level up, as well as to prevent injuries.

The main purpose of writing this book is to promote tennis and perhaps, this may help to create interest in many more children and young adults to play and improve their game of tennis; and a good proportion of them can advance to become *great tennis players* at the national and international level.

2) TO PROMOTE YOGA

The other main purpose of writing this book is also to promote Yoga to help people in sports and fitness and generally maintain good health; and to be involved in the sports of their choice, such as tennis, for a long time, even in the autumn years of their life, without incurring injury.

After compiling the CPR system of Tennis and yoga for sports, I asked myself 'What makes me qualified to write about tennis and yoga?'

Regarding Yoga, I taught Hatha Yoga, pranayama and meditation both with my father and independently for many years, on a volunteer basis. I practice *Raja yoga* and *Gnana yoga* (yoga of wisdom)

My specific qualification is that of a Siddhar Yogi. Siddhar is a mystic who is proficient in the practice of Raja yoga and Gnana yoga. Traditionally, four types of yoga are described:

Karma yoga---yoga of action with the right attitude
Bhakti yoga---yoga of devotion
Raja yoga---yoga of meditation (Hatha Yoga practice of a*sanas or poses is, in fact, a preparation for meditation)* and
Gnana yoga---yoga of wisdom.

However, they all have the same ultimate goal of realizing the *changeless Truth,* which in turn, is the basic substratum of all the four divisions of yoga and all things in Nature. For the same reason, one may practice one or more of the above four. Yoga in Sanskrit means *union;* so, one may abide in *the changeless truth,* through any one or all of the above four.

With regard to tennis, I am a recreational player, still playing in my seventies at a reasonably good level. Due to medical career in my younger years, I have not actively taken part in competitive tennis. However, I was a senior champion for one year at the Berkeley Tennis Club (in 2008).

Now-a-days, in my retirement, I win sometimes and I lose sometimes; when I win, I accept it; and in the same way when I lose, I accept it---in tennis as well as generally in life.

HOW TO USE THIS BOOK

FOR TENNIS

1. For tennis, refer back to the details given in the text of the book again and again, both before and after playing a practice game of tennis or ball-machine or back-wall practice, so that you can understand how focusing on the *reference points* given in this book, help the shot making as well as the movements in the tennis court. It is as though the tennis coach is always there giving details of the instruction needed.

FOR YOGA

2. For the Yoga poses, have a minimum of poses to do, as a routine every day, including a few warm-up poses and *Surya Namaskaram.* Then add two or three poses from the remaining poses described in this book; and keep rotating these additional choices of poses, in order to keep the daily routine to a reasonable time. It is important you do not strain and push yourself beyond the limits, dictated by your body. Lying down for one or two minutes after each set of yoga poses will let the body and mind enjoy the benefits and effects of the poses.

Staying fit and healthy, and playing with *good technique* is important. It does not guarantee winning all the time; but it does help to prevent injuries in tennis. In the same way, living with *Kindness* and *Good Intentions* in thought, word and deed is important. It does not guarantee winning and success in life all the time; but it does help to prevent un-happiness and injuries to the mind. That is both my purpose and qualification in writing about tennis and yoga for the benefit of others.

1. TENNIS MADE EASY

THE DYNAMIC CPR SYSTEM

The player, the tennis ball and the position of the racquet are continuously moving and hence, *variable*, creating millions of possible scenarios. So, it is nearly impossible to learn the movement and technique for each situation separately, to execute the shots successfully. So herein is described a dynamic system of *CONSTANT POINTS OF REFERENCE* – CPR.

In this Dynamic CPR System, 'CPR' stands for Constant Points of Reference. *Dynamic* is defined by Webster's Dictionary as, "relating to energy, motion or physical force; always active or changing". *Constant* is defined by the same dictionary as "staying the same, not changing; happening all the time or very often over a period of time".

At the outset, these two words may appear contradictory, dynamic meaning 'active and changing' and constant meaning 'not changing'. In fact, they are complementary to each other.

'Dynamic' refers to 1) the body of the tennis player who is always moving and changing position and 2) the tennis ball that is also continuously moving.

'Constant' refers to certain points of reference, described in this system that remain constant in relation to 1) the body of the player and 2) the tennis ball and 3) the tennis court.

For example, the tennis ball is always moving and changing, during the game and so is *dynamic*. At the same time, the six-o-clock position on the ball, for example, is *constant* at the time of contact with the racquet. So, the CPR–constant point of reference– for the tennis ball is both constant and dynamic at the same time.

This system was developed with the following *facts of life in tennis,* in mind.

Fact #1. Even though the tennis court and the net are *static* and do not move, the ball, the players and the racquet are constantly moving - hence *dynamic*. Together, they create countless possibilities in any given moment. So, the movement of the racquet in a certain way may work sometimes and not at other times. Variations mentioned above and in the 'Introduction' are the reason for the inconsistency in the game of tennis for all levels of players.

In the dynamic CPR system, the point of reference is *constant*, for any given shot or serve; and at the same time, it is *dynamic* because it moves with the player and the ball – thus increasing the consistency. When consistency increases, the confidence-level increases and there is more room to increase the speed of the swing.

Fact #2. In any given situation, for any shot or serve, the player cannot remember six different points, not even five or four. So in the dynamic CPR system, there are only a maximum of three points to remember in any given situation, of which two of the three will become automatic as a *reflex* with practice; and there will be *only one constant point* of reference to *focus*, that is dynamic, i.e. moving with the ball and the player.

Fact #3. With any system of learning and improving the game of tennis, if the player tenses up, that is the beginning of disaster for any level of playing. So, a simple approach of *meditation* technique, of *watching the normal breath* is recommended. Normal breath may be slow or fast, depending on the amount of running during the game; the player does not try to increase or decrease the rate or depth of the breathing; merely being aware of the breathing, at that moment, is what is recommended, and will prevent the tensing.

An ancient text book on yoga, *Hatha Yoga Prathipika* says that the mind is controlled by 'Prana' or breathing; Prana is 'Life-Energy'.

THE READY POSITION

The "Ready Position" applies to all levels and all shots.

There was a book published in 1977 titled *"Watch the Ball, Bend Your Knees, That'll Be $20 Please!"* The twenty-dollar fee for a tennis lesson dates the book to a by-gone era, but the advice given in the title still holds true.

For the sake of completion, we should add a third one to the above advice, i.e., 'hold the racquet with both hands' with the non-dominant hand holding the neck of the racquet. So, following the 'not more than 3 points-format' we discussed earlier, the ready-position involves

1. -bending your knees, with the feet about two shoulder widths apart and the feet on the balls of the feet in the front half of the feet. This is a good habit to develop early on. It helps in every aspect of tennis, especially to move towards the ball, as needed; and to move the body weight from the back foot to the front foot, while hitting the ball.

2. -holding the racquet lightly with both hands, with the dominant hand at the handle and the non-dominant hand (the left hand for a right-handed player and vice versa) at the neck of the racquet, and

3. -looking at the ball: Looking at the ball is not

mere watching the ball; you are supposed to track the trajectory of the ball, to the right side or left side etc., to track the ball and to be able to see the lines on the ball while hitting the shot or the serve.

SLICE SHOTS: Another example of the tracking is in the slice shots. Usually, if the opponent is slicing from *his or her* left to the right side, then the ball will bounce up from *your left to the right side.* The degree of change of direction will of course vary.

The ready position becomes automatic with practice; and so, there is no thinking involved about the above three points. In fact, in the whole game of tennis for all levels, it is important to play spontaneously, using various reference points described in the system of CPR; and so there is no thinking involved, only *observing* the reference-points and executing the appropriate shots. Thinking always leads the player to *past* events in the game, such as double faults, or to the *future*, such as winning the game or the set, instead of focusing on each shot, one at a time.

IMPORTANCE OF DRILLS

It is essential to have practice drills with a coach or at the ball-machine regularly, in order for
1. the 'ready position' and
2. the weight transfer from the back leg to the front

leg during shots, to become automatic and also for the movements of the player in the court etc., to become automatic.

Then the player will be able to *focus* on the *reference points* described in this dynamic CPR system, with everything else happening automatically. Some of the examples of such automatic actions, required in the game of tennis are as follows.

THE FOOT-WORK AND THE WEIGHT-TRANSFER

The CPR or the reference point for the foot-work is the ball itself. If the ball is seen coming to the right side of the player, the shoulder turns to the right side and along with the shoulder, the right foot moves sideways, forwards or backwards, as needed to reach the contact with the ball. For a right-handed player, this creates the forehand shot and for the left-handed player, it creates a backhand shot.

If the ball is seen coming to the left side, the left foot moves similarly, along with the shoulder turn to the left side. These rules apply to both regular shots and the volley.

If the ball is coming directly at the receiver, the player needs to turn the shoulder to the right side or left side and move away from the ball. The above steps are described to give a mental picture of the movements; however, focusing on the reference point should bring you to the correct spot automatically.

It is important to realize that this helps the weight

transfer from the back leg to the front leg, creating the foundation for the shot. Keeping the knees bent, helps this process.

Immediately after the shot, the front leg pushes to return the player to an 'optimal position'. What is an optimal position?

THE OPTIMAL POSITION

The position of the player is dynamic and hence moves accordingly. In an *approach shot* for example, the player's optimal position moves from the baseline to the service-box or near the net, for a volley. For single's game, it is in the middle of the base-line and for doubles it is in the corresponding half of the court, near the base-line. Based on the location of the ball during the game also, the optimal position keeps moving. The reason for the description of the optimal position, is for the player to return to or move towards the 'optimal position', by pushing on the front leg, after each shot.

SHOULDER TO CHIN POSITION

Another fundamental point of reference is the 'Shoulder to Chin Position'. I learned this from Lynne Rolley, the head-coach at Berkeley Tennis Club, in a clinic for overhead shots. Then I applied it to other shots and found it useful, as described below.

The shoulder to chin movement should happen as a unit-turn of the body.

In forehand shots, the left shoulder for a right-handed person (and the right shoulder for a left-handed player) is brought to the chin, thus twisting the body towards the ball, immediately followed by the left hand pointing at the ball, with the pointing hand moving slightly forward, as described in the reference point system for forehand shots. This subtle movement of the pointing hand, along with the *shoulder to chin position,* looks obvious when you observe the forehand shot by players like Roger Federer and Novak Djokovic.

The shoulder to chin movement should happen as a unit-turn of the body. Similarly, in the backhand shot, the shoulder of the racquet hand is brought to the chin, when the racquet is taken back in preparation for the backhand shot.

In the 'serve', the left shoulder for a right-handed player (and vice versa for the left-handed player), is brought to the chin, as a continuation of the tossing movement, with the shoulder turn. This brings the left shoulder above the level of the right shoulder; and the opposite happens when the racquet is made to swing up to the ball: the racquet shoulder goes up, as described in the serve technique later.

Similarly, in the overhead shot the left shoulder (the non-racquet side) is brought to the chin, before the racquet-swing.

The shoulder to chin position is as fundamental and important as the three points mentioned under the ready position. Similar to the ready position, the shoulder to chin position also becomes automatic with practice, so that the CPR system can be followed to bring about focus and consistency.

SPLIT STEP
The split step is one of the important basic skills

that needs to be developed early on. The split step needs to happen before every shot, either to the full extent when possible, or a glimpse of it when there is not enough time. It should happen when the ball leaves the opponents racket. What is needed then is a reference point that is constant and the player can use that as a "cue" to do the split step. Such a *reference* point is the opponents racquet itself. That means that when a player notices the opponents racquet moving, the split step should happen at the same moment. That will give the player enough time to respond to the trajectory of the ball.

BREATHING

It is important to develop the habit of breathing throughout the game of tennis, in order to have endurance. For example, in the forehand the inhaling should start when the body turns towards the ball along with the shoulder to chin position and the non-racquet hand pointing to the ball. The exhaling should happen while hitting the ball. This exhaling enhances the speed as well.

Similarly, in the backhand inhaling starts when the body turns towards the side of the ball, and the exhaling should happen while hitting the ball.

In the serve, the inhaling should start in Step 2 with the knee-bend and the shoulder turn (the trophy-pose) and the exhaling should happen while hitting the ball.

In the volley, inhaling should start during the movement of the body towards the ball, and the exhaling should happen while hitting the ball.

TENNIS AND YOGA

The concept of observing and being aware as well as the spontaneous action come from the yoga discipline in which we are advised to be constantly 'aware'.

Our emphasis here is based on paying attention and focusing on the reference points for the corresponding shots. During the execution of any shot in tennis, the eyes should be glued to the ball and the appropriate reference point on the ball.

REFERENCE BOOK

The reader is encouraged to refer back to these pages, as a reference book, again and again to gain understanding and to make it useful to improve the game.

FOCUS VERSUS STRATEGY-----IS IT A CONUNDRUM?

If the emphasis is on the focusing on the reference point on the ball, some valid questions may arise, such as, when to observe the movement and position of the opponent and how to form a *strategy* without observing the opposite side of the court. The answer still lies 1) in focusing on the ball; not merely on the player's side of the court but on the opposite side of the court. 2) following the trajectory of the ball from the racquet of the opponent to the player's side of the court, all the way to the appropriate reference point on the ball and 3) in assessing the movement and position of the opponent players with the peripheral vision, until the ball reaches this side of the net.

However, once the ball is on the player's side of the net, the focus has to be on the reference points on the ball, 100%, as described below.

(In order to get to the heart of the CPR system right away, the section on the *Grips* on the racquet will be discussed separately.)

THE FOREHAND

The Dynamic CPR system for the beginner level as well as for all levels includes the following:

Reference Point #1.
The First Point of Reference is the Left Hand. The left hand (for a right-handed player) comes off the neck of the racquet---from the Ready Position---when the left shoulder moves to the chin and *then* the *left hand* Points the ball coming towards the player. The point of contact of the ball by the racquet is where the hand is pointing, at about the hip-level usually, slightly in the front; however, the level may vary, depending on the position of the ball and point of contact needed for the forehand shot.

This, "automatically" does three important functions;

1) The upper body is turned sideways.

2) The racquet is taken to the back comfortably, for a speedy acceleration of the racquet.

3) The point of contact is never too early nor too late, with the hand showing the optimal point of contact,

a) in relation to the timing and

b) never too far away nor too close to the player, in relation to the location of the contact.

Also, the non- dominant Hand pointing the ball, coming towards the player at about the hip-level usually, makes the player go to the right position in the court. This is the first Constant Point of Reference. The pointing hand moves each time, with the direction of the ball coming towards the player- thus a dynamic CPR. It is constant because the pointing hand stays with the player.

THE POINTING HAND PULLS BACK:

As the racquet moves to the contact point, for the forehand shot, the Pointing-Hand, namely the left hand for the right-handed player and vice versa for the left-handed player, is pulled to the side of the body to catch the neck of the racquet again *above the non-racquet shoulder*, preparing for the next shot. This movement of the Pointing Hand, pulling back to the side twists the upper body and carries the racquet forwards, creating the follow-through of the shot automatically. This also increases the speed of the racquet tremendously.

Reference Point #2.

The Second Point of Reference is the Six-o-Clock Position of the ball; this refers to the point of contact of the racquet with the ball, for a forehand shot. The pointing hand, described above, with practice, *automatically,* brings the player to the right position and points the ball. So, the only reference point to focus for the player is this 6-clock position of the ball, to execute the forehand shot.

For the topspin shot, the racquet swing is from below the ball-- low to high.

For the backspin shot, the racquet swing is from above the ball-- high to low.

Reference Point #3.

For the Inside-Out and the Outside-In shots, the reference point on the ball, is the same with the following qualification: for the inside-out shot, the point of contact is slightly inside of the six-clock position; and for the outside-in shot, the point of contact is slightly to the outside of the six-o-clock position. The position of the player is very important for both the shots as described here.

The position of the player and the point of contact with the ball will change to help both inside-out and outside-in shots as follows:

For the Inside-Out shot, the point of contact is

slightly behind the player; so the player's body is turned more towards the back fence, with a slight delay in the contact with the ball. The *reference point* is slightly Inside of the Six-O-Clock position, as mentioned above. (In a way, it is a Cross-Court shot, from the ad-side of the player to the ad-side of the opponent).

For the Outside-In shot, the point of contact is slightly in front of the player, with the contact with the ball, happening more quickly. The *reference point* is slightly Outside of the Six-O-Clock position.

The typical Cross-court shot is very similar to the Outside-In shot, except it starts with the player in the dues-side of the court and the ball ending in the dues side of the opponent.

The above description is based mainly in relation to the contact with the ball, because the *constant point of reference* for the forehand is the Six-O Clock position of the ball.

There is now a necessity to clear a confusion in terminology here; some teachers refer to the Outside-In shot as Inside-In, when it is described in relation to the location of the player, rather than the reference point on the ball. For example, with the player in the ad-side, the shot ends up in the dues-side of the opponent. The same shot is sometimes, also referred to, as 'down the line'. Whereas, there is no multiple terms used for the Inside-Out shot.

THE BACKHAND

Compared to the forehand, everything in the backhand occurs a split second sooner in time; that means the contact point for backhand is slightly more *forwards* than the contact point for the forehand; and the shot is executed closer to the body, in space. So, the player needs to reach the position, that is closer to the ball in time.

Similarly, in 2-handed backhand also, the player has to be closer to the ball than for the forehand shot.

CONSTANT POINTS OF REFERENCE--CPR for the backhand addresses
#1. The Body of the player and
#2. The tennis ball

Reference Point #1
The reference points for the Body of the player are
    A)   the side fence and
    B)   the back fence of the court,

A) The player, as soon as he realizes the ball is coming to the backhand, turns his body towards *the side fence*. For the right-handed player, the body turns to the left side-fence and vice versa.

B) The racquet hand moves towards *the back*

fence, to the left side of the hip, (to the hip-pocket, as Lynne Rolley would say); and the knee-bend of the back leg, as one unit, starts the body weight in the back leg.

The racquet-swing starts from the back in the closed position for top spin, and open position for the back-spin shot.

Again, in relation to the body of the player, the front foot, that is moving as per the above description, begins to land towards the *location of the landing of the ball,* coming to the backhand side. The player may observe the transfer of the body-weight from the back foot to the front foot, during the above movement.

The racquet-swing continues swiftly for the backhand shot from the back, with the racquet face *closed,* to the reference point of *seven-o-clock* position of the ball.

The racquet-head ends up in front and above the level of the head of the player. The difference is, for the topspin shot, the racquet ends up in line with the racquet-arm; and for the back-spin shot, the racquet ends up at right angles–90 degrees–to the racquet arm.

The non-racquet arm is extended to the back for balance, at the same time as the racquet arm ending up in the front.

GRIP is of course eastern backhand grip or continental grip, for the backhand shots.

Generally speaking, the eastern backhand grip is used for the topspin shot and the continental grip is used for the back-spin or slice shots.

In the two-handed backhand, the left hand assumes eastern forehand grip for the left hand, above the right hand; and vice versa for the left-handed player.

Reference Point #2.

The reference point for the Tennis Ball:

The only point of reference is the Seven-O-Clock position of the ball.

The player hits the ball approximately at the 7-clock position of the ball, both for the top spin and back-spin shots. For the top spin, the racquet contacts the ball, from below the ball; and for the back-spin, the racquet contacts the ball, from above the ball.

As described in the beginning, the reference points with regard to the fence become a reflex with practice and become automatic movements; and the only reference point, the player has to focus is the Seven-O-Clock position on the ball.

For the inside-out and outside-in shots, the position of the player is more crucial than anything else. So it does not require a separate reference point. For the inside out shot, the contact is made, slightly to the inside of the 7-clock position of the ball. For the outside-in shot, the contact is made, slightly to the outside of the 7-clock position.

All backhand shots in relation to the reference point of the ball are, in a way, Outside-in shots!

THE SERVE

Now for the all-important Serve, the reference points are a little more complex and so we need to analyze the serve mechanics in detail.

The beauty of tennis lies in the serve because it is one shot that is 100% in the control of the player.

Reference Point #1.

The net post of the tennis court is the first reference point– a static point of reference– the right sided post for the right- handed player and the left sided post for the left-handed player.

Reference Point #2.

The second reference point is the inner side of the back-foot of the player. The inner side (or the medial side in medical terminology) is the space between the sole of the foot and the upper part of the foot. This is a dynamic point of reference, because the inner side of the back-foot moves with the player.

THE READY POSITION FOR THE SERVE:

The two reference points above are used for the ready position.

1. The front foot is pointing at the corresponding net post.

2. The inner side of the back foot is pointing towards the service box, where the ball is supposed to

land.

3. The ball is held softly and comfortably at the distal part of the flat area of the palm (not on the fingers); and the neck of the racquet is held gently above the hand holding the ball.

The description above applies to both the dues-side serve and the ad-side serve.

In fact, all the descriptions of the serve mechanics, described here will apply to both the dues side and the ad-side serve. That is what makes this CPR (constant points of reference) system consistent and simple.

THE REFERENCE POINT FOR THE TOSS

The *Reference Point* for the toss is found as follows:

The Ready Position is an ideal time to find the *Reference Point for the Toss*.

To begin with, find the *reference point* for the toss for the serve, in the ready position, with the body-weight on the front foot.

There are two lines involved in finding the reference point for the toss, in order to have a consistent toss and consistent serve.

DON'T WORRY; you do not have to take a 'Geometry 101' class in the middle of the tennis game, because this reference point will become automatic with practice, once you become familiar with the concept.

THE TWO IMAGINARY LINES

Line One: Draw an imaginary line between the corresponding net post and your shoulder. Swinging the racquet towards the net post facilitates to form this line.

Line Two: If you must only remember one point, it should be your belly button that will move with you, regardless of your position. Draw an imaginary line from your belly button to line One, at 90 degrees to the plane of the body. You may have to turn the upper body accordingly, in order to face this *reference point* at 90 degrees to the plane of the body. Where line Two meets line One, is the reference point for the toss. This will somewhat vary, depending on the position of the body. That is why this will always be a constant point of reference for the toss, regardless of the position of the body.

You may bounce the ball one or two times, at the reference point for the Toss to occur. With practice, the reference point for the toss will become automatic, for any position the player assumes for the serve.

Again, this is another place, the idiosyncrasy of the player may show up, for example, as multiple bounces, before the serve.

This point is a Dynamic Reference point, moving with the 'Ready Position' of the player and never changes and is always Constant, in relation to the player, when the above guidelines are followed. For example, the toss in the dues side and ad side will follow the Reference Point of the Toss, mentioned above, even though your position changes.

The GRIP is *continental* for the Serve.

From the ready position, the Serve consists of 3 steps as follows:

Step One--RHYTHM LEADING TO TOSS

(For the sake of better lighting for the photographs of the Serve, the author is standing inside the court, facing the back fence. So, the reader is advised to ignore the court configurations.)

The racquet hand is holding the racquet lightly.

Notice the tossing arm being straight and the body moving forward for the toss and the racquet lag.

THE RHYTHM AND IDIOSYNCRASIES

The player starts with the racquet and the straight tossing arm together. Everyone should have a rhythm; this is where the rhythm starts. There are as many idiosyncrasies of rhythm as there are tennis players. So following the reference points described above will give consistency to the serves, in spite of the idiosyncrasies.

As the player gently lifts the toes of their front foot, the body weight moves from the front foot to the back foot.

When the player then sways forwards with the front of the front foot moving towards the floor, the body weight moves forwards, giving momentum for the tossing arm to go up, releasing the ball above the head, at the Reference point of the toss, described above as the junction of the two imaginary lines.

The toss is the most important part of the serve; if the toss is consistent, then the serve is consistent. There are many, many descriptions of the toss. That shows not only the importance of the toss in a serve, but also, there is no perfect system that works all the time. So, herein, we have come up with a system after many, many hours of research and practice, that will give a consistent toss, thereby leading to a consistent serve.

It is highly recommended to keep the tossing arm gently outstretched and straight to the reference point, where the two imaginary lines meet., so that the toss is from the shoulder; and not from the wrist. The arm being straight, without the bending of the elbow, cannot be emphasized more, for getting a consistent toss and consistent serve. At the time of releasing the ball, at about the eye level also, the whole arm remains straight, so that the tossing arm moves up at the shoulder; and not at the elbow or wrist.

As a part of the rhythm, it is recommended to start the swing of the tossing arm in front of the *reference point for the toss;* and bring the arm down to the reference point of the toss; and then swing the arm up for the toss. It helps to have a *consistent toss*.

The details of the toss are described in both Step One and Step Two, the Toss occurs at the end of the Step One and continues on, in the Step Two, as a continuous movement.

Step Two: TOSS LEADING TO COIL DOWN AS ONE UNIT; AND THE RACQUET LAG

The racquet arm is beginning to move back with supination; notice the knee-bend before the body springs up. The body is almost turned behind; racquet arm is in supination. The racquet shoulder is below the level of the opposite shoulder.

As the racquet moves up *quickly* from behind the back to hit the ball, the non-racquet arm comes down.

The Lag: Tracing back to the rhythm of Step One, when the tossing arm left the company of the racquet, the racquet lagged behind with the racquet arm moving up laterally ever so slightly and bending the elbow acutely, in preparation for the Racquet Swing in step three. The intent here is for the player to be merely aware of the racquet lag.

COIL DOWN: The Tossing arm goes up, making the body to turn behind by

A) the bending of the knees and

B) shoulder turn of the racquet arm, getting ready to uncoil, when the ball makes a turn downwards.

The Tossing Arm stays up, with the *Shoulder moving to the Chin.*

The body weight is loaded in the back leg. The Lag and the Knee bend and the tossing arm staying up are simultaneous, as one unit, even though they have to be described separately; and this part of the rhythm of serve blends with the next step of the racquet swing as follows:

Step Three– **UNCOIL UPWARDS LEADING TO THE RACQUET SWING**

Notice the forearm, still in supination, ready to pronate at the time of contact, any moment, to create the 'whipping action.' Notice both feet beginning to lift off the ground. The racquet shoulder is now above the level of the opposite shoulder.

The front foot is landing inside the court and the racquet is coming down after the 'whipping serve action.'

(In the photographs of the serve, above, the reader is reminded of the reversal of court configuration with the server facing the back fence from inside the court, for better lighting of the photographs.)

The racquet should be held very lightly, as though one is holding a baby quail bird or a baby chicken-- the bird is held with enough grip to prevent flying away and at the same time not to choke it-- and one may practice it by holding the racquet with the thumb and index and middle fingers, leaving the other two fingers free, to get the feeling of holding lightly.

The *shoulder-turn and* the racquet swing upwards with the player *jumping up* to hit the ball at the Reference Point (described below separately) together form the step three of the serve.

A. The knee-bend and the Shoulder Turn:

The knee-bend creates the shoulder-turn, similar to the chin-moving to shoulder, and coils down the body further.

B. Jumping Up:

Jumping up with the racquet-swing up *uncoils the body*. The racquet arm remains in *supination i.e., the racquet face is facing sideways,* until the arm pronates at the time of contact with the ball.

The player lands inside the court with the front foot (the left foot for the right-handed player) and the racquet swing ends to the left side.

The RACQUET SWING-- SUPINATION AND PRONATION

The racquet swing consists of two parts.; however, the swing is one swift and smooth action upwards.

1. THE SUPINATION --- AS THOUGH PULLING THE EAR BACK

In the first part, the forearm supinates, taking the racquet behind the ear, *as though,* you are pulling the ear backwards-- right ear for the right-handed player and the left ear for the left-handed player--with the body turning behind by the bending of the knees. The racquet dangles below the hand, holding the racquet.

2. THE PRONATION

The purpose of the Supination, described above, is mainly to facilitate the Pronation, described here. In the second part, while the player jumps, the racquet, held very lightly by the player, swings upwards towards the ball that is taking the turn downwards. The forearm *pronates*, while making connection with the ball.

The Pronation in this second part is again made easy and automatic by swinging at the Constant point of reference of the ball described below following this description of 'Supination and Pronation'.

Aiming the racquet swing from the Supine position of the forearm to the One-O-Clock point of reference of the ball brings about Pronation of the forearm automatically. Further details are given below in the description of CPR--the constant point of reference of the ball for the serve.

The first and second parts of the Racquet Swing, namely the supination and the pronation, together make one constant reference point, even though they are described separately for convenience of expression.

REASONING

Supination and pronation are opposite actions. A pronated forearm cannot pronate further. So, the forearm needs to supinate first to facilitate natural pronation at the time of contact of the racquet head with the ball, in the serve.

SUPINATION and PRONATION–DEFINITION

The words supination and pronation need clarification here. Both these words can be understood, when you start with a person lying down flat, with the face and palms of the hands facing up; this is called the supine position.

Here the forearm is said to be in supine position.

When the palm is facing down on the floor, in the same lying down position, the forearm is said to be in the prone position.

The biceps muscle is the most powerful supinator. When one supinates the forearm from the palm down to the palm up position, notice the biceps muscle to contract. When the palm facing up, is turned, facing down, it is called Pronation.

CPR– CONSTANT POINT OF REFERENCE– for the BALL for SERVE

This reference point is considered as a Constant and at the same time, Dynamic reference point, because it moves with the ball (as opposed to a static reference point, such as the net post).

The reference point of the ball for the serve is One-O-Clock position of the ball, for the racquet to swing at the ball, at the apex of the swinging motion of the racquet with the player jumping up. Reaching up for the One-O-Clock Position of the Ball makes the forearm Pronate automatically.

This One-o-clock position is, in actuality, a Seven-to- One-O-Clock Movement of the racquet on the ball, giving the 'peeling the orange skin' effect, like a top-spin shot. The peeling the orange skin off the ball continues over the ball, automatically, when the player aims to the baseline of the court, while swinging the serve motion.

For a slice serve, the reference point to aim, is Nine-o-clock to Two-o-clock position on the ball.

THE TIMING

The timing for serving motion varies with the technique used for serving. For the technique, described above, the timing is herein described.

The server uses this timing, as follows, mentally.

The Three Steps of the Serve is a *Chain of Events* as follows:

1. RHYTHM *Leading* TO TOSS---ONE unit of time
2. TOSS *Leading* TO COIL DOWN---ONE unit of time
3. UNCOIL UP *Leading* TO SWING THE RACQUET ---ONE unit of time

ONE: (RHYTHM LEADING TO TOSS) is meant for starting the Rhythm to release the Toss as described above. The starting of the Rhythm is given 'One Unit of Time', even though the 'Rhythm' continues on, in the steps two and three of the serve also.

TWO: (TOSS LEADING TO COIL DOWN) is used for the lag of the racquet;   and

1) The toss leading to coil down of the body, described above and includes taking the racquet arm to the side to the shoulder level, with acute bending of the elbow; and for the knee-bend and shoulder turn of the racquet arm, as a *unit-turn* of the upper body.
2) The player is merely aware of the racquet dangling down, i.e., the racquet-lag.

THREE: (UNCOIL UP LEADING TO SWING THE RACQUET) is used for the jumping up and Swift Racquet Swing with Supination followed by Pronation to the Reference Point on the Ball, as described above.

If the server wants to use only number for each unit of time, use the following:

ONE: (RHYTHM AND TOSS)

TWO: (RACQUET LAG AND COIL DOWN– includes Shoulder-to-Chin Position)

THREE: (UNCOIL UP AND THROW TO THE REFERENCE POINT ON THE BALL)

If the player wants to use *Key Words,* instead:
Toss
Lag, knee-bend
Jump Up.

Or simply,
T
L
J

Here, T is for rhythm and toss

L is for Lag of the racquet (knee-bend and shoulder-turn are automatic)

J is for Jump-up (pronation of the arm is automatic, when the racquet reaches up from the 'racquet-lag to the contact point on the top of the ball)

Different choices of using numbers or letters are given here because the *Serve* is such a complex part of tennis; and different players have varying strengths and weaknesses in the movements for the serve.

So the player is advised to try the different systems

of numbers or letters and stick to the system that works well, individually.

THE SERVE AND BASEBALL PITCHING

The racquet swing is often aptly compared to the Base Ball Pitching, as the Pitcher takes the ball to the back and throws the ball, forwards, with pronation.

Besides the Base-Ball pitching action, the concept of *Supination followed by Pronation is* also used in Boxing and Karate, where the striking arm, flexed in elbow with supination is released swiftly to throw a *punch* with pronation.

Foot-Ball throwing and Cricket-Ball bowling are other examples of the use of the same concept. The reader should by now understand the importance of learning this concept of *Supination followed by Pronation* described here.

THE KICK SERVE

All the above reference points apply to the Kick Serve also except as follows:

For the kick serve, the reference point on the ball is Twelve-O-Clock position on the ball i.e., Peeling the ball from Six-O-Clock to Twelve-O-Clock position on the ball.

The toss is a little closer to the body and above the head of the player.

The grip moves from the continental position slightly towards the eastern backhand grip.

SERVE-PRACTICE AND NEWTON'S THEORY OF GRAVITY

Similar to other aspects of the game, the serve also needs thousands of repetitions to improve consistency. Some players feel that practicing the serve especially the toss, with used balls may be different from playing with newer balls in a match.

However, the fact is that all the tennis balls when tossed up, will come down at the same speed, irrespective of the condition of the ball, whether used or new, as long as the air resistance is not significantly different. The balls will accelerate down at the same speed, due to the force of gravity.

Galileo proved with experiments, all objects of any

size or mass come down towards the center of earth at the same speed. Newton later proved that all objects come down towards the center of earth at a fixed rate of 9.8meter/second square, when there is no air resistance, i.e., in a vacuum.

The air resistance may play a part in the speed of the ball coming down. However, the wind factor due to the air resistance applies to all the tennis balls, whether new or old.

THE OVERHEAD

The description of the Overhead technique follows the above description of the serve, because the overhead shot resembles the serve in many ways. The player turns sideways facing the ball, and turns the chin to the shoulder of the non-racquet arm with that arm going up; while the racquet arm raises up, similar to the serve. The player follows the ball, moving to, just behind the ball; then strikes the ball, similar to a serve, at about the One-O-Clock position. Here again, the One-O-Clock position of the ball is the CPR-the reference point.

It is important to mention here, if the player has to move backwards or to either side, the movement is with the body turned sideways; and secondly, in small steps especially close to reaching the ball.

The GRIP is continental, similar to the serve.

THE VOLLEY

The Ready Position: The racquet is held with both hands, with the non- dominant (non-racquet) hand holding the racquet at the neck of the racquet, with straight arms, similar to the Ready Position of the Forehand and Backhand.

FOREHAND VOLLEY

The main difference between the forehand volley and the backhand volley is the orientation of the shoulder. In the forehand volley, there is no shoulder turn, so ball is hit in front of the player. In the back-hand volley, there should be a shoulder turn automatically and the ball is hit in front of the player.

The GRIP is continental, similar to serve and overhead; eastern backhand grip also will work.
The racquet face is very slightly open; and the racquet faces the target in the court, while hitting.

The CPR points of reference for the volley are:

1. The eyes are used to eye-ball the ball so that the eyes and the racquet-hand move towards the contact point at the ball-level.

2. The racquet punches the ball with a backspin; and the movement of the racquet is short and swift. It should be emphasized here that there is no place for swinging the racquet in Volley and so the racquet is never taken to the back.

BACKHAND VOLLEY

Notice the Racquet head, held up with no back swing, starting the movement above the level of the ball. The left hand is still on the neck of the racquet.

The body is moving towards the ball.

By turning sideways, in the backhand volley, the body-weight, moving to the foot that is closest to the ball, gives the volley the strength needed. The foot that is closest to the ball lands on the floor or preferably, the feet keep moving as the case may be, as the volley shot is made. It is no exaggeration, when it is said that the movement of the foot makes the volley.

The difference in the backhand volley is, both hands stay with the racquet most of the time, if not all of the time. This makes the player turn the body towards the ball along with the front foot moving to the corresponding side and the body-weight moving to the target.

Thus, the non-racquet hand holding the neck of the racquet, as long as practical, functions as the reference point, directing the body to turn towards the ball in the back-hand volley automatically.

BACKHAND HIGH-VOLLEY

The racquet-head held straight up, to the level of the "High-Volley" ball; the body is moving to the ball.

The racquet head is moving forwards. (And then downwards– not shown.)

SOME VARIABLES

Some of the Variables need to be added here, such as an Approach shot and Half-Volley.

APPROACH SHOT
For example, an Approach shot is very useful in moving towards the net to facilitate a Volley shot. The main point in the approach shot is the swing is much shorter and there is no backswing both for forehand and backhand shots. The Grip can be continental.

HALF-VOLLEY
Another Variable is the Half-volley. In Half-volley, the contact with the ball is made right close to the ground, right after the ball bounces. The grip is the same, namely eastern forehand grip for the forehand and backhand grip for the backhand.

It should be noted here that a teacher/coach or a parent who understands the importance of focusing on the different reference points given in this CPR system of points of reference, can make it easier to learn for the player; and a good coach can make the game of tennis very enjoyable!

2. THE GRIP

The various grips commonly used are:
1. Eastern forehand grip
2. Eastern backhand grip
3. Continental grip
4. Some players use semi-western grip, especially for the topspin forehand shot.

The grip should be held lightly, to enable a natural swing of the racquet.

THE OCTAGON OF THE HANDLE

The handle of the racquet is octagonal; there are four flat sides and four slanted sides between the four flat sides. For the sake of describing the various grips, mentioned above, the sides can be numbered as follows:

Hold the racquet in front with the racquet face *facing sideway,* as shown in the picture..

#1: When the racquet is held in front with the racquet-face *facing sideways*, the top flat side is #1.

#2: Moving clockwise, the slanted side is #2

#3: The flat side is #3.

#4: The slanted side is#4, and so on and so forth up

to #8 on the slanted side to complete the 'octagon' of the handle.

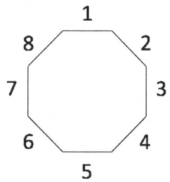

Shows the end of the handle with the racquet face, facing sideways.

CONSTANT POINT OF REFERENCE for GRIPS

Using the numbering of the eight sides of the octagon of the handle, the description of each grip is made simple. Use the *knuckle* of the index finger as the Constant Reference Point on the different sides of the handle, described in the *octagon*.

Even though the wrist is not used in shot-making, a slight extension or bending back of the wrist helps to create a more 'natural' swing of the racquet. This prevents you from holding the racquet like a hammer.

EASTERN FOREHAND GRIP

In the eastern forehand grip, the knuckle of the index finger is on the #3 side of the handle; this is usually described as ' the handshake' grip. Note the line connecting the knuckles is at at about the 15 to 30-degree angle.

As the name implies, this grip is used for forehand shots; these can generate a powerful topspin, using the CPR system of reference points, described earlier. Here's the sequence of movements:

The non-racquet hand points to the ball at the contact point. The racquet swings at the 6-o-clock position of the ball.
The racquet head ends to the left of the player, for a right- handed player.

EASTERN BACKHAND GRIP

In the Eastern backhand grip, the knuckle of the index finger is on the #1 side of the handle. This allows the player to swing the racquet like a frisbee, to reach the outer side of the ball at the 7-o-clock position of the ball.

CONTINENTAL GRIP

In the continental grip, the knuckle of the index finger is on the #2 side of the handle.

This is a very versatile grip because the continental grip is recommended for

1. Serving
2. Volley and sometimes, Half-Volley
3. Slice and Drop shots
4. Backspin or slice with follow through
5. Backhand shots also can be played with a continental grip, rather than the eastern backhand grip, described above.

SEMI-WESTERN GRIP

In the semi-western grip, the knuckle of the index finger is on the #4 side of the handle. Some players prefer this grip for forehand topspin shots.

This concludes the 'Tennis /CPR System' and 'The Grip'.

3. YOGA APPLICATIONS FOR SPORTS AND FITNESS

BODY MECHANICS

YOGA Asanas keep the body nimble and strong.

The *asanas* (postures) described here can be used to prepare for sports activities, such as Tennis, as well as for general well-being to keep the body flexible and strong.

It is a good practice to do the yoga postures every day at about the same time, followed by Pranayama breathing. In case of not being familiar with Pranayama breathing, deep breathing and/or aerobic exercise can be helpful. To reiterate the importance of regular practice, consistency is more important than the duration of practice on a daily basis.

The importance of preventing problems with regular yoga practice is stressed in the following text; and a few notes are added to the descriptions of the poses, with prevention in mind.

The BODY-MIND CONNECTION

The influence of Mind over the Body has been

well documented as "The Mind-Body Connection". On the flip side of the coin is the influence of the bodily movements and poses over the brain and its chemistry and the resultant changes in the mind. I call this the "The Body-Mind Connection".

It has been discovered recently that neurotransmitters send messages through trillions of synapses across billions of neurons. The neurons are the nerve cells of the body and are responsible for the function of the mind. The influence of the neurotransmitters across the neurons makes the delineation between body and mind less and less remarkable. They allow the body and mind to become a unified system for all practical purposes.

Yoga masters of India have, of course, studied the effects and benefits of yoga practice for many centuries both for emotional well-being and as a foundation for spiritual enlightenment.

In the 19th century in 1884, William James, an American philosopher published a controversial article that raised the probability that physical actions can elicit corresponding emotion; rather than the emotion causing the physical action. For example, when a person runs away from a bear, it is the immediate reaction of running away that causes the emotion of fear, rather than the fear causing the physical action of running. In other words, it is not *fright and flight* as it is commonly known; it is probable that it is *flight and fright.* It raised a controversy that lasted through the next century.

It was not until the late 20th century and early 21st century, further research and publications have shown the role of poses and bodily movements in changing brain chemistry and emotions. It likely coincided with the introduction and popularity of yoga in the Western Hemisphere and studies involving the yogic system were being reported in increasing numbers.

These studies show the benefits of yoga in the neuro-endocrine system at the biochemical level and anatomical level. They also indicate large scale benefit among the general population.

RECENT STUDIES ON YOGA PRACTICE

Using magnetic resonance spectroscopic imaging, Chris Streeter, MD, an assistant professor of psychiatry and neurology at Boston University School of Medicine (BUSM) and Harvard affiliated McLean Hospital, reported that practicing yoga may elevate levels of brain gamma amino butyric acid(GABA), the brain's primary inhibitory neurotransmitter (published in the May 2010 issue of the Journal of Alternative and Complementary Medicine).

This is the first study to show an association between Yoga practice, increased GABA levels and decreased anxiety.

The findings suggest that the practice of Yoga can be considered as a possible treatment for depression and anxiety. The World Health Organization reports that mental illness constitutes up to fifteen percent of diseases in the world. Such depression and anxiety are typically associated with low GABA levels and are often successfully treated with pharmaceutical agents that increase GABA levels.

In the methodology of Streeter's study, two randomized groups of healthy subjects were followed for a 12week period. One group practiced *Yoga* three times a week for one hour per session; the other group *walked* for the same period of time. At the end of twelve weeks, the researchers compared the GABA levels of both groups, before and after their final 60minute session.
Each subject was also asked to assess his or her psychological state at several points throughout the study.

Those who practiced Yoga reported a more significant decrease in anxiety and greater improvement in mood than those who walked. Over time, positive changes in these reports were also associated with "climbing GABA levels".

In 2010, Dana Carney and others from Columbia University and Harvard University, published an article in Psychological Science, showing that testosterone and cortisol levels changed, when certain poses were held for a total of two minutes (not unlike the method of staying in the Yoga poses for a certain length of time).

In this study, forty-two subjects---26 females and 16 males---were randomly assigned to the 'high-power' or 'low-power' poses. The subjects were told that the study was about the science of physiological recordings and was focused on how placement of electrocardiography electrodes above and below the heart could influence data collection--- to avoid the influence of subjective feelings on the results, namely the hormone levels.

The subjects' bodies were then posed by a researcher into high power and low power poses. Each participant held two poses for one minute each (total of two minutes).

The subjects' risk taking was measured with a gambling task; feelings of power were measured with self-reports.

Saliva samples were taken before and approximately seventeen minutes after the 'power pose' manipulation, to measure cortisol and testosterone levels. The poses were harvested from the lexicon of non-verbal communication.

In the 'high power' pose, the subjects were instructed to keep the feet up on the desk with their fingers intertwined behind their heads (expansive pose, taking more space) for one minute. They were then told to keep their hands on the table with legs spread out for one minute.

In the 'low power pose', the subjects were instructed to sit in a chair, with legs together and hands held together on the thighs (a contractive pose, taking less space) for one minute. They were then told to stand with legs crossed and arms crossed over each other for one minute.

The study was done in the afternoon to control for diurnal rhythms in hormones.

The results showed that posing in high power displays caused elevation of the dominance hormone testosterone, reduction of the stress hormone cortisol, and increases in behaviorally demonstrated risk tolerance and feelings of power. Posing in low power displays caused the opposite of the above findings.

These findings suggest, according to the lead author, 'that the effects of embodiment extend beyond emotion and cognition, to physiology and subsequent behavioral choice'.

Kirk Erickson, a neuro-scientist from the University of Pittsburgh and others from the University of Illinois found that people 60 to 79 years old who completed a six month program of *walking briskly* on a regular basis showed an increase in the size of the hippocampus and levels of BDNF---brain derived neurotrophic Factor–comparable to those normally found in people almost two years younger.

The hippocampus normally shrinks by 0.5 percent each year, starting at age 40.

There were two control groups in the study--one group did toning and stretching exercises and another did nothing; the control groups showed no brain changes.

The above three studies provide objective data at the biochemical level and anatomical level.

Studies in 2011 and 2012 show the benefits of Yoga at a larger scale, as follows.

In a multi-centered randomized controlled trial, professor David Torgerson, of the University of York's Department of Health Sciences, did a study funded by Arthritis Research UK. The study provided an evaluation of a specially developed twelve-week group yoga intervention program, in comparison to conventional general practitioner (GP) care alone, for patients with chronic or recurrent low back pain.

This was the UK's largest ever study of the benefits of Yoga and was published in the journal Spine.

Back pain is estimated to cost the UK National Health Service(NHS) £1.37 billion and the health care sector UK £2.1 billion a year. It is also one of the UK's most common conditions; about 2.6 million patients seek advice from their GP for back pain each year.

Researchers concluded, "while Yoga has been shown as an effective intervention for treating chronic and low back pain, this study showed its cost effectiveness. Back pain is also a major cause of work absenteeism, which leads to a productivity loss to society. The 12 weekly group classes of specialized Yoga are likely to provide a cost-effective intervention for the treatment of patients with chronic or recurrent low back pain".

They further concluded that with £300 per patient for 12 Yoga sessions, there is about 70 percent probability of yoga intervention being cost effective. This probability will likely be higher, if the cost of health care goes higher or the cost of yoga sessions becomes lower or both.

In another study on chronic low back pain, the largest U.S. randomized controlled trial of Yoga to date (published by the Archives of Internal Medicine, as an 'on line first' article on October 24th 2011), 228 adults in six cities in Washington state were randomly assigned to three groups.

The first took 12, weekly 75 minute classes of Yoga. The second took 12 weekly stretching exercises. In the third group, they were assigned to read a comprehensive self-care book called, The Back-Pain Help Book. The subjects had moderate back pain and relatively good mental health.

1. In the Yoga group, the Yoga principles were adapted to individual physical condition, with modifications for people with physical limitations. The Yoga sessions included breathing exercises and deep relaxation at the end.

2. The stretching classes used 15 different stretching exercises, including stretches of the hamstrings and hip flexors and rotators. Each was "held for a minute and repeated once"(similar to the holding of poses in Yoga), for a total of 52 minutes.

Karen J. Sherman, PhD. MPH, the lead author "in retrospect, realized that these stretching classes were a bit more like Yoga than a more typical exercise program would be", because the stretching poses were held in position for a certain length of time, similar to Yoga Practice.

3. The third group followed the self-care book, 'The Back-Pain Help Book', with neither Yoga nor stretching.

The class participants received instructional videos and were advised to practice at home for 20 minutes a day.

The researchers found Yoga classes more effective than a self-care book; and the stretching classes (which, in retrospect, were similar to Yoga exercises), were also more effective than the self-care group after 12 weeks. Back related function was better and symptoms were diminished with Yoga classes; and clinically important benefits, including less use of medications, lasted at least 6 months for both Yoga and stretching, with thorough follow up of more than 90 percent of participants.

This study was funded by The National Center for Complementary and Alternative Medicine, a part of the National Institute of Health.

Another randomized controlled clinical trial from Charite-University in Berlin, Germany was published in the Journal of Pain in 2012. The study showed that Yoga was an effective treatment for chronic neck pain and also provided benefits of improved psychological well-being and quality of life. Of the 53 volunteer patients from different centers in Germany and Austria, 25 were assigned to the Yoga group and 23 were assigned to self-care exercise.

They completed a standardized questionnaire at the beginning of the study, after four weeks and after ten weeks. The Yoga sessions consisted of Iyengar Yoga, in which props such as blocks and belts are used to fit individual capacity. The Yoga postures were also tailored to fit an individual's medical problem.

The results showed a significant and clinically important reduction in pain intensity in the Yoga group. The authors reasoned that yoga might enhance both the toning of muscles and releasing of muscle tension. Relaxation responses, therefore, could reduce stress related muscle tension and modify neurobiological pain perception. The researchers concluded yoga can be a safe and effective treatment option for chronic neck pain.

REVIEW OF THE STUDIES ABOVE

1) IMPORTANCE OF HOLDING THE POSE

A review of the above studies suggests that holding the pose in the same position for a minimum of one minute results in a beneficial change in the hormonal levels in the research study by Dana Carney and others.

The study at Washington state found that stretching practice that was held for a certain time gave the same benefit of relief of pain as the Yoga practice in which the poses are traditionally held in position for a certain length of time. The third group that did not do either Yoga or stretching with holding the pose, did not experience relief of the low back pain.

In the research study by Dana Carney and others from Columbia University and Harvard University, the subjects that held the expansive or high power pose with a total holding time of two minutes showed an increase in testosterone hormone levels and a decrease in cortisol levels. The reverse was seen in the contractive or low power pose, with a decrease in testosterone hormone levels and an increase in cortisol levels. Such an increase in cortisol levels are typically seen in 'stress', described by Hans Selye.

The common denominator in the above studies that showed significant changes either in the hormone levels or relief of pain, appears to be the *holding of the pose* for a certain length of time. It did not matter whether the poses were called 'stretching' or 'expansive pose' or 'contractive pose' or 'Yoga practice'; they all produced the expected changes, as long as they were held for a certain length of time, similar to the Yoga practice which typically recommends holding the pose.

> To quote Shakespeare in Romeo and Juliet,
> "What is in a name? That which we call a rose
> By any other word would smell as sweet"
> (Juliet 2.2.43-44)

So, in the practice of Yoga poses, described below, it is advisable to hold the pose for as long as possible to enjoy the benefit of the practice.

2) SIDE EFFECTS OF DRUGS

Side effects of many of the drugs used in the above studies can be either minimized or eliminated by adding Yoga practice to the care of some medical conditions, such as depression, anxiety, low back pain and chronic neck pain, as shown in the studies. For example, aspirin and non-steroidal anti-inflammatory drugs, such as ibuprofen, usually prescribed for back pain and neck pain and taken for a prolonged period can cause gastritis and peptic ulcers.

3) COST OF MEDICAL CARE AND LOSS OF WORK-DAYS

It was also clearly shown by the above studies that

the cost of medical care and the loss of work-days can be minimized on a large scale by adding Yoga practice to the care of certain chronic conditions.

Some studies already prove the benefits of meditation in treating hypertension; thus, lowering the dose of drugs or removing the need for drugs. Many of such studies were done, using a type of meditation called TM, transcendental meditation, in which there is silent repetition of a
'mantra' word or words.

However, more large- scale studies are needed to pinpoint the exact type of yoga practice needed for many other medical conditions, especially disorders where the underlying cause is unknown, such as autoimmune diseases and arthritis, as a therapy in the milder and early stages, as well as complementary to other forms of therapy in lowering the dose of pharmaceutical agents, thus reducing the side-effects as well as the overall cost of healthcare at the national level.

The DAILY ROUTINE OF YOGA PRACTICE

Due to time constraints in the busy schedules of the modern-day lifestyle, it may not be possible to perform all the following yoga postures, every day. However, it is recommended to do a few asanas, individually selected from the list below on a daily basis and add one or two more as time permits. It is recommended to add Surya Namaskaram–the Sun Salutation to the daily routine practice.

1. Warm-up asanas
2. Balancing asanas
3. The Sun Salutation–Surya Namaskaram
4. The Warrior pose–Veera Badrasana
5. The Core Exercises– Ardha Matsyendrasana and other Poses
6. The Shoulder Stand–Sarvangasana
7. The Fish pose–Matsyasana
8. The Bridge pose–Setu Bandha Sarvangasana
9. The Plough pose-Halaasana
10. Modified Shoulder stand–Vipareeta Karani
11. The Back-Stretching pose–Paschimottanasana
12. The Pigeon pose–Eka Pada RajaKapotanasana

The Relaxing Pose is recommended at the end of any routine practice of Yoga. The relaxing pose is called Savaasana

A WORD OF CAUTION

Similar to any form of exercise, it is advisable to consult with a physician before starting yoga practice, especially if you have medical problems such as hypertension, heart disease, glaucoma or diabetes or during pregnancy.

BEFORE THE MATCH

Everyone is different and so it is an individual preference as to how much and what kind of exercise preparation to do before a match. However, just before the match, such as a tennis match, a lengthy session of exercise or yoga practice is not recommended. A few warm-up and balancing asanas, described below plus a short period of aerobic exercise, the morning of the match are all that is needed as a tune up.

Regular Yoga practice should be done on a daily basis, either before or after a shower in the morning or evening, as a routine.

AEROBIC EXERCISE

YOGA PRACTICE is not a substitute for aerobic exercise, such as brisk walking, jogging, running, cycling or playing tennis. In Tennis, about 45 minutes of singles play is considered equivalent to 90 to 120 minutes of doubles.

Studies have shown that even moderate exercise, such as brisk walking, for 30 minutes a day can prevent diabetes, as well as maintain normal blood sugar in patients with diabetes.

It is recommended to maintain the heart rate that is an average of 70 to 75 percent of an arbitrary number of '220 minus age' for a minimum period of 30 minutes a day, for 5 to 6 days a week, depending on the age and condition of the person.

In order to achieve the average of about 70% of "220 minus age" one may sprint to bring the heart rate to about 80% to 90% of "220 minus age", for a short time and then slow down to bring the heart rate to 60% of the above arbitrary number. For example, for a 40 years old person, "220-40" is equal to 180 and 70% average heart rate to maintain for that person is 126 beats per minute.

For the purpose of aerobic for racquet sports, such as tennis, racquet ball and squash, it is recommended to do short bouts of sprinting to about 80 to 90percent of "220-age" for 1 or 2 minutes, and slow down to achieve about 60% of "220-age", to mimic the running needed in such games.

Alternately, in another method, especially for cardiac aerobic exercise the heart rate is maintained at a range of about 70 to 85 % of "220-age", during the aerobic exercise time of 30 minutes, with about 10 minutes of warm up before and 2 to 5 minutes of cool down after the aerobic maintenance time. This is also recommended for endurance, as a training for marathon running.

Aerobic exercise should be done for a minimum of 150 minutes a week. This is known to prevent medical problems, such as diabetes, hypertension and heart disease.

YOGA PRACTICE can also be aerobic, when a shortened version of sun salutation is done rapidly 108 times; it should only be done under the guidance of a yoga teacher. Some advanced yogis practice such a routine.

YOGA PRACTICE and aerobic exercises generally are considered
complementary to each other; and as mentioned above, Yoga practice promotes general well-being and prevents medical problems and sports injuries. It carries some therapeutic benefits as well, as will be described in the following text.

A few warm up poses and exercises, in order to stretch the muscles and loosen the major joints of the body and a few balancing-asanas are recommended before doing the sun salutation-- Surya Namaskaram that will be described later.

1) WARM-UP ASANAS

THESE WARM-UP ASANAS CAN ALSO BE DONE BEFORE A TENNIS MATCH, BESIDES THE USUAL QUADRICEPS STRETCH AND CALF STRETCH

1. BUTTERFLY ONE: BADDHA KONASANA

Bring the soles of the feet together, in the sitting position, and hold the feet together with both hands.
Bring the feet as close to the body as possible.

Move the elbows out and bring the forehead towards the feet and breathe normally.

If the body is flexible enough, one may bring the forehead to the feet gradually.

Remain in this pose for 6 breaths or as time permits.

2. BUTTERFLY TWO: POORNA TITALI ASANA

In a variation of the above Baddha Konasana pose, after holding the feet together with both hands, flap the knees as fast as comfortable.

This will help to loosen the hip joints and their muscles. The aim is to bring the knees to the floor, gradually.

3. HAMSTRING AND GLUTEAL STRETCH

Lie down. Bending both knees, raise both feet off the floor.

Bring the right ankle over the left knee.

Clasp both hands in front of the left knee, by passing the right arm under the right calf muscles.

Pull the left knee towards the body, gently and firmly.

Feel the stretching of the Right hamstrings and gluteal muscles. Remain in the pose for 3 to 6 breaths.

Repeat the same with the other leg.

4. TRIANGLE POSE– TRIKONASANA–STEP ONE

TRIANGLE POSE–TRIKONASANA
INCLUDING THE VARIATION ONE

Stand facing forward, with the feet about 3 feet apart.

Raise the arms in front, parallel to each other and spread them to both sides like wings, inhaling.

Turn the right foot to the right side about 30 degrees.

Then take the right hand to the right foot, with the left arm going up. Both arms are in a straight line.

Look up at the left hand. The left palm is facing forward. Notice the right knee bending slightly. Remain in the pose for 6 breaths.

Here is a tip to keep the knees straight; before moving the right hand to the right foot, push the hip to the left side as much as possible. This will facilitate, keeping the knees straight, when the right hand is taken to the right foot.

Stay in this position for 6 breaths, inhaling and exhaling. Return the arms to the sides, in a straight line. Repeat the same on the other side.

Variation 1 :

Bring the right hand to the right foot, as described above; then take the left arm to the right side over the left ear, until the arm is parallel to the floor.

Similarly, breathe in and out for 6 breaths. Feel the stretch of the ribs and the side muscles. Straighten the body and bring the arms to the sides.

Repeat the same on the other side.

Variation 2 :

Start with the feet about three feet apart and with the arms to the side, breathing in.

Bend forward and twist the upper body to the right side, with the left hand touching the right foot and the right arm stretching upwards in a straight line and the face looking up at the right arm.

Stay in this position for 6 breaths, inhaling and exhaling. Then straighten up.

Repeat the same on the other side.

With practice, one should be able to place the right palm to the outside of the left foot and vice versa. One may also do this pose rapidly, if it is done as a part of aerobic exercise.

5. DOUBLE ANGLE POSE– DWIKONASANA

Start in the standing position, with the feet hip-width apart.

Take the arms to the back and interlock the fingers and extend the arms up, until the arms are at right angles to the back, while bending forward at the hip.

The arms are raised up as much as possible. Bring the face towards the knees, keeping the knees straight.

Stay in this pose for six breaths and reverse the steps to the standing pose.

This pose strengthens the muscles around the shoulder blades and also the muscles of the pelvic diaphragm. Thus, when practiced every day, it can prevent prolapse of the pelvic organs in women; and is especially recommended after child birth.

Alternately, keep the face parallel to the floor, looking forward, in the final position.

The final position forms two angles, one between the legs and the trunk and the other between the back and the arms; hence the name Dwikonasana, the double angle pose.

2) BALANCING ASANAS

BALANCE IN TENNIS WILL HELP ALL MOVEMENTS IN THE COURT AND IN THE SERVING MOTION; WILL ALSO HELP TO PREVENT INJURY

The following two balancing asanas are described, with the main purpose of possibly preventing a sports related injury. In the beginning, they give balance and steadiness to the body; and gradually, these poses also help to develop a balanced mind, removing anxiety and stress.

1. ONE LEGGED PRAYER POSE– EKA PADA PRANAMASANA.

Stand with feet together and focus on a point in front of the face at about the level of the eyes to help the balancing of the body.

Shift the body weight to the left leg.

Bend the right knee and place the sole of the foot on the inside of the left thigh by holding the ankle and pulling it up, so that the heel is close to the perineum and the right knee is towards the right side.

Alternately, the top of the foot may be placed on the top of the opposite thigh, as shown in the picture, similar to *Ardha Padmasana*

Pull the lower abdomen in and stiffen the left leg muscles.

Once balance is achieved, the hands holding the ankle can be released and brought to the chest or above the head for the prayer position, hence the name PRANAMASANA.
EKA PADA means one leg.

Start with six breaths and increase the duration of the pose as long as possible.
Repeat the same on the other side.
Reverse the steps to come out of the pose.
In a variation of this pose, the arms may be taken above the head and held in the prayer position.

2. GARUDASANA– Eagle Pose
This pose is recommended for intermediate to advanced level, since it requires a fair amount of flexibility of the joints. As with other poses, 'forcing' the body to achieve the pose is not recommended.
Stand straight with feet together and bend the knees slightly.
Place the right leg over the left knee and twist around the left leg, with the right foot resting on the calf of the left leg. If the right foot cannot reach the calf, rest

the foot on the floor, next to the left foot.

To provide balance, focus on a point on the floor in front of you.

Bring the arms parallel in front and bend the elbows.

Place the right elbow over the left elbow and twist the forearms around each other. Bring the palms together, resembling an eagle's beak, hence the name Garudasana.

Bend the left knee as much as possible and keep your focus on a point on the floor.

Hold the position for six breaths in the beginning, and gradually increase the duration, holding as long as possible.

Reverse the steps to come out of the pose.

Repeat the same on the other side. Reverse the steps to come out of the pose.

This pose helps to loosen the joints of the arms and legs also, besides improving balance, as mentioned above.

3) THE SUN SALUTATION
SURYA NAMASKARAM

The traditional Surya Namaskaram will be first described, followed by other postures that can be inserted into the Surya Namaskaram.

The Surya Namaskaram has a few variations, depending on the different schools of yoga; but it still manages to maintain a certain uniformity in the number of poses and in the effects achieved.

The following poses should be done slowly and comfortably without straining, to avoid injury. Each pose can be paused for three to six breaths, before going to the next pose.

The Surya Namaskaram or Sun Salutation consists of a series of twelve postures, as follows:

1. PRAYER POSE – PRANAMASANA

Stand with feet parallel at hip-width, with palms together at chest level and eyes closed, for a short time, until you can feel the mind calming down.

2. RAISED-ARMS POSE– HASTA UTTANASANA

Raise the folded palms, above and behind the head, breathing in slowly.

Follow the inhale or exhale with each posture for the duration of either the in breath or the out-breath.
Generally speaking, breathe in during extension of the spine and body; and breathe out during flexion.

3. HAND TO FOOT POSE – PADAHASTASANA

Bring the hands down to the feet or ankles, whatever is possible, breathing out slowly.

Then place the two hands on the floor, outside the feet, at the same level as the feet.

Contract the abdominal muscles at the end of breathing out.

4. EQUESTRIAN POSE– ASHWA SANCHALANASANA

Take the right foot backwards as much as possible, looking up and breathing in.

Stay in this pose for three to six breaths. It is helpful to bring more blood supply to the pelvis and pelvic organs.

5. THE MOUNTAIN POSE– PARVATASANA
DOWNWARD FACING DOG– ADHO MUKHA SVANASANA is the popular name for this pose.

From the equestrian pose, bring the left foot also backwards, next to the other foot and bring the head to the space between the two arms in the front, breathing out.

Stay in this pose for three to six breaths. It is also considered to be a modified *SIRSHASANA–head stand pose*–bringing more blood supply to the head and neck.

You may keep the feet on your toes, raising the heels up slightly.
To stretch the calves and hamstrings more fully, push one heel down, while lifting the other heel up,

alternately. Then firmly place both feet on the floor.

The legs and the back form the two sides of the 'mountain', hence the name PARVATASANA.

Stay in this pose, breathing in and breathing out slowly.

OPTIONS FROM PARVATASANA

There are many options that can be done from Parvatasana, such as warrior poses, pigeon pose, child pose etc.,

Two of such possibilities are added here, to be done as a sequence of *Surya Namaskaram,* if one is able to do them comfortably. Otherwise, you may drop the knees to the floor from Parvataana and proceed to the step 6–*Ashtanga Namaskaram.*

5.A: THE SLANTED PLANK

Bring the body almost parallel to the ground, by dropping the hip down and moving the upper body forwards, from the 'downward-facing dog'-Parvatasana pose until the body is straight like a *slanted plank.*

Breathe in during this pose.

Dropping the knee down, proceed to Baalasana or the child pose as described below.

5.B: THE CHILD POSE– BAALASANA

Drop the knees to the floor and take the hips back

to sit on the heels, with the soles of the feet facing up.

When the knees are brought close together, with the right big toe on top of the left big toe, it is called the VAJRASANA or diamond pose.

In BAALASANA, the knees are moved out wide in order to place the forehead on the floor in front, breathing out, forming the child pose. The arms are stretched out in front.

MODIFIED BAALASANA

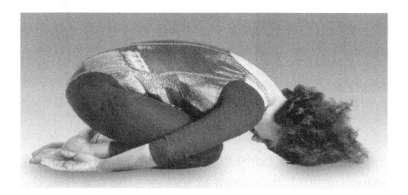

In a 'variation', introduced by the author's father, the arms are brought backwards to lie next to the legs; this allows for even more relaxation.

This is a good pose to rest in, as needed.

Breathe in and breathe out during the pose.

6. SALUTATION POSE– ASHTANGA NAMASKARAM

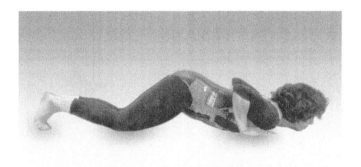

From the child pose, crawl the upper body forwards, until the chest and chin touch the floor, with the chin between the hands.

In this position, the toes, knees, chest, chin and hands touch the floor. The breath is held in retention during this pose.

7. COBRA POSE– BHUJANGASANA

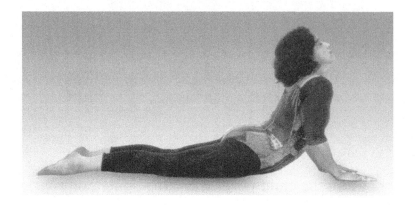

Breathing in from this pose, take the head and chest up, with the navel (belly button) and lower part of the body touching the floor, forming the cobra pose. Keep the elbows close to the body. It is important to have the navel touching the floor for a good extension of the spine.

8. THE MOUNTAIN POSE–PARVATASANA OR DOWNWARD FACING DOG– ADHO MUKHA SVANASANA

From the cobra pose, raise the hip up and bring the head to the space between the arms, breathing out, forming the Parvatasana (*'the downward facing dog'*) again.

Breathe in and out in this pose. Stay in this pose for three to six breaths, similar to the step five– Parvatasana. It brings more blood supply to the head and neck.

9. EQUESTRIAN POSE– ASHWA SANCHALANASANA

From the Parvatasana, shift the body weight to the left arm to make it easier to move the right foot. Bring the right foot forwards to the space between the two hands in the front, breathing in.

10. PADAHASTASANA

Now shift the body weight to the right arm and move the left foot forwards, next to the right foot.
Straighten the knees, with the hands or fingers touching the feet, forming the Padahastasana again.

Then breathe out.

11. HASTA UTTANASANA

Take both hands up above and behind the head, breathing in, forming the Hasta-Uttanasana.

12. PRANAMASANA

Bring the palms to the chest, forming the Pranamasana.

Close your eyes, breathe out and feel all your worries fly away.

Repeat the same 12 steps above for the opposite side. Now for the left side, bring the *left foot* backwards *first*, instead of the right foot first in the step four, to start the *Equestrian* pose from the *Padahastasana*.

Similarly, in the step ten, take the left foot forwards, to start the Padahastasana again.

This now completes 'one cycle'.

One may stay in each of the twelve steps for three to six normal breaths and continue on to the next step. This gives full benefit of the poses.

One may do two or more cycles of the Sun Salutation, up to twelve cycles, as time permits.
Traditionally, an experienced yogi may do a shorter version of the Surya Namaskaram 108 times, rapidly.

VARIATIONS ADDED TO SUN SALUTATION:

1. UPWARD FACING DOG
In the first cobra pose, raise the knees up, standing on the toes, and look up thus forming the Upward facing dog pose.

2. ONE LEGGED DOWNWARD FACING DOG– EKA PADA PARVATASANA
In this variation, one leg is raised up from the 'downward facing dog' pose, keeping the hip and shoulders square, by not twisting the trunk to the side.
The author found it is more easily achieved by starting in the PLANK position and lifting one leg, simultaneously moving the trunk back to the 'downward facing dog' position; and place the sole of the other foot on the floor by lowering its heel.

Repeat the same on the other side. Remain in the position for 6 breaths on each side.

MODIFIED SCORPION POSE– VRISCHIKASANA

In a further variation of the above, raise one leg up, as above and bend the knee, stretching the hip without twisting as follows:

From the PLANK position, raise the right foot up, as high as possible.

Then bending the knee and raising the leg up further, move the foot towards the head, stretching the corresponding hip.

This will complete 'THE MODIFIED SCORPION POSE'.

Repeat the same with the left foot. Stay in each side for 6 breaths.

Then reverse the steps and return to the standing PRANAMASANA pose.

For a variation of the SCORPION POSE– VRISCHIKASANA, follow the same steps as above; and in the final pose of the above, simply drop the knee of the straight leg, to the floor; and stretch the raised-up leg, as much as possible, without twisting the hip.

Repeat the same with the other foot.

4) THE WARRIOR POSE— VEERA BADRASANA
HELPS ALL THE ASPECTS OF TENNIS BY STRENGTHENING ALL THE FOUR EXTREMITIES AS WELL AS THE RIB MUSCLES

VEERA BADRASANA– ONE.

Stand with both feet together. Raise the arms up above the head and slowly bring them down towards the feet, similar to PADAHASTASANA, and place the hands on either side of the feet. Bending the knees, swing one foot all the way to the back; turn the back-foot 45 degrees and line up the heel to the heel of the front foot. The front knee is bent, taking care not to bend beyond the level of the toes. The back leg is straight. Raise both arms up close to the ears. Stay in this level for six normal breaths.

VEERA BADRASANA – TWO.

From the above posture, stretch the arm that is same side as the front foot, forwards and the other arm backwards.

Stretch like the wings of a bird.

Make sure the *front knee,* does not travel beyond the front toes, to avoid injury to the knee.

Stay in this posture for six normal breaths.

VEERA BADRASANA– THREE

From the above pose, take the back arm to the back of the thigh and the front arm up, stretching the ribs, facing up.

Stay in this posture for six normal breaths.

Feel the ribs stretch as much as possible.

VEERA BADRASANA– FOUR

From the above pose, bring the front arm to the front thigh, resting the arm on the thigh above the knee.

Take the back arm to the front, above the head, as shown in the picture, now stretching the ribs.

Stay in this pose for six breaths.

Return to the Veera Badrasana One, stretching both arms up. Bending forwards, place both hands next to the feet.

Bring the back-foot forwards next to the front foot.

Now repeat all the four variations in the opposite side by swinging the foot that was in the front in the above description, to the back.

Similarly, place the back foot at 45-degree angle, lining up the two heels in the same vertical line.

Repeat all the four steps of the Veera Badrasana, similar to the description above.

5) CORE EXERCISES

The core muscles include the muscles of the upper body and pelvis.

It is important to have strong core muscles for any sport, especially tennis.

Core muscles are used in every aspect of tennis.

Most of the yoga asanas described here under 'YOGA APPLICATIONS' do help to develop a strong core. However, two poses are separately described here.

CORE 1.
ARDHA MATSYENDRASANA

HELPS BOTH FOREHAND AND BACKHAND, BY IMPROVING FLEXIBILITY OF THE WHOLE SPINE FROM THE SACRUM TO THE TOP OF THE CERVICAL SPINE.

ALSO IMPROVES THE CORE STRENGTH.

This asana is named after a Siddhar named MATSYENDRANATH.
A Siddhar is a Mystic whose perfection in the

practice of yoga and wisdom has reached beyond the level of the mind and is able to maintain an equanimity, so that he is not swayed by the dualities of the ups and downs of the life and the reactions of the mind.

Examples of dualities of life include sweet and bitter, pleasant and unpleasant, good and bad, pride and humble, pleasure and pain, likes and dislikes, and in the far ends of the spectrum, *depression* and *manic* phases of the mind.

The ancient text book on Yoga, Hatha Yoga Pratidipika was written by Swatmarama, the disciple of Gorakhnath, who was the expounder of Hatha yoga.
Gorakhnath was the disciple of Matsyendranath

Ardha MATSYENDRASANA is a very versatile asana. The variation number three, described below, with the leg stretched in front, can be done as a warm up asana also in the beginning of the practice session.

VARIATION ONE:
Sit on the floor with the legs stretched out in front.
Bend the right knee and place the right foot under the left buttocks.
Place the left foot on the outside of the right knee. The left foot is facing the front and the sole of the right foot is under the left buttocks.
Twist the whole upper body to the left so that the

right elbow can be taken to the outside of the left knee, gently pushing the left knee.

The right fore-arm is either holding the outside of the left thigh, or is pointed upwards.

The left hand is taken to about the middle of the back and placed on the floor for support, to enhance the spinal twist.

Breathe normally and stay in this position for six breaths in the beginning, and gradually increase the duration, to as long as comfortable, for about 20 to 30 breaths.

Reverse the steps and release the legs one by one.

Repeat the steps for the opposite side for the other side. This is one cycle. It will be enough to do one cycle for each session.

VARIATION TWO:

Sit on the floor with the legs stretched out in front.

Bend the right knee and place the right foot under the left buttocks.

Place the left foot on the outside of the right knee.

The left foot is facing the front and the sole of the right foot is under the left buttock.

Twist the whole upper body to the left and instead of placing the right elbow on the outside of the left knee, the right arm is wrapped around the left knee, embracing the left thigh.

The left hand is taken to about the middle of the back and placed on the floor for support.

Breathe normally and stay in this position for six

breaths in the beginning, and gradually increase the duration to as long as comfortable, for about 20 to 30 breaths.

Then reverse the steps and release the legs one by one.

Repeat the steps for the opposite side for the other side. This is one cycle. It will be enough to do one cycle for each session.

VARIATION THREE:

For beginners who cannot bend the knee acutely as described above, the right leg can be kept straight and the left foot placed on the outside of the right knee.

The left foot is facing the front.

Twist the whole upper body to the left so that the right elbow is taken to the outside of the left knee, gently pushing the left knee.

The right forearm is either holding the outside of the left thigh, or is pointed upwards.

The left hand is taken to about the middle of the back and placed on the floor for support.

Breathe normally and stay in this position for six breaths in the beginning, and gradually increase the duration to as long as comfortable, for about 20 to 30 breaths.

Then reverse the steps and release the legs one by one.

Repeat the steps for the opposite side for the other side. This is one cycle. It will be enough to do one cycle for each session.

This asana helps to improve the flexibility of the spine and may prevent problems related to osteophytes of the vertebra and spinal stenosis. It can also relieve symptoms of sciatica and back muscle spasm at the lumbar area.

This is a very useful pose for tennis for the forehand, backhand and serve, all of which require twisting of the body. This is also a useful pose for any sport that requires a flexible, twistable spine.

As with all other asanas, people with medical problems should get clearance from their physician. These asanas are not recommended for people with slipped disc, or during pregnancy.

CORE 2.
REVOLVING ABDOMEN POSE
JATHARA PARIVARTANASANA

Jathara means abdomen and Parivartana means revolving.

HELPS BOTH FOREHAND AND BACKHAND SHOTS OF TENNIS BY
BUILDING THE CORE STRENGTH

1. Lie down facing up; raise one leg up from the

hip 15 degrees; then bring the other leg up 15 degrees also, keeping the other leg up; breathe three breaths.

Keeping the legs up, raise the legs to 30 degrees; breathe three breaths. Bring the legs down slowly and repeat six times or as time permits.

Raise the legs up, same as above; then raise the legs to 45 degrees and then to 90 degrees slowly.

With the arms spread out laterally like wings, slowly take the legs laterally from the hip to one side to the winged arm.

Breathe in and out six times.

Then move both legs up to the other side slowly to the other winged arm.

Breathe in and out six times.

Repeat the Parivartanasana six times or as time permits.

3. Perform the same above posture, with knees bent. You will find it easier to do with the knees bent. It is best to do both ways, for optimal effect.

Repeat six times or as time permits.

CORE 3.
CAT STRETCH POSE
MARJARI ASANA

HELPS BOTH FOREHAND AND BACKHAND BASELINE AS WELL AS VOLLEY SHOTS OF TENNIS, BY IMPROVING FLEXIBILITY OF SPINE.

It is also known as Dog and Cat Pose.

Make a bridge with palms and knees and the lower leg on the floor. The arms are vertical from the shoulder; and the trunk is horizontal.

Breathing in slowly, depress your back, to extend the spine from coccyx (the lower end of the spine) to the neck and look up–the dog-pose.

Then Breathe out slowly, arch your back up, to flex the spine from the neck to the coccyx and contract the rectum and the head drops down to, between the arms–the spine goes up like a cat stretching.

Repeat 6 times or as time permits.

CORE 4.
THE CAMEL POSE
USHTRASANA

HELPS TENNIS SERVE AND OVERHEAD

Sit on the heels of the feet with the knees bent, and the knees hip-width apart as in VAJRASANA.
Now stand on the knees, with the upper body and thighs supported by the quadriceps and gluteal muscles.

Raise the arms up and bring one arm at a time back to hold the heels of the feet.

Breathe in and out normally 6 times or as time permits.

Then reverse the steps to come out of the posture.

This helps to develop extension of the spine as in tennis serve or overhead.

CORE 5.
THE BOW POSE
DHANURASANA

FOR TENNIS SERVE AND OVERHEAD

This is also a good pose for the extension of the spine, that helps in tennis serve or overhead.

Lie down on the belly with the arms on the side.

Bend both knees, raising the lower legs.

Hold the ankles with the arms stretched towards the feet and gently pull the thighs off the floor, raising the chest up and extending the spine.

If the arms cannot reach the ankles, you may hold the lower legs, wherever it is comfortable to reach.

Hold the posture for 6 normal breaths and slowly release the ankles and bring the chest back to the floor

6) THE SHOULDER STAND– SARVANGASANA

SARVANGASANA AND MATSYASANA
Sarvangasana and Matsyasana are described together, because Sarvangasana should always be followed by Matsyasana.

SARVANGASANA

IMPROVES ALERTNESS IN TENNIS THROUGH CARDIOVASCULAR SYSTEM AND THYROID STIMULATION; ALSO IMPROVES MOBILITY, BY INCREASING THE VENOUS RETURN FROM LEGS AND PELVIS

It is also known as all-limbs posture.

My father used to say, "Sarvangasana is considered the 'mother of all yoga poses', because it involves all the sections of the body."

It is a very powerful asana, especially for the cardio-vascular system, increasing the venous return from the lower parts of the body, and with the body upside down, the movement of the diaphragms during breathing, massaging the heart and lungs.

This asana also helps the endocrine system, especially the thyroid and parathyroid glands.

Lie down flat on the back with elbows to the sides of the body.
Bend the knees up.
Then raise the legs up by raising the hips first, then the lower back and the upper back upwards. Straighten the legs up.
Pushing with both palms and the fingers on the floor will help to raise the hips and will facilitate raising the legs. Support the hips with both palms.
Then, gradually, move the hands up to the lower back and then upper back, as the legs and the trunk move up.
The shoulders stay on the floor, hence the name 'shoulder stand'.
The hip, lower back and most of the upper back are held up vertically with both hands supporting close to

the midline.

The chin is pushing on the chest.

Support the back with both hands and stay in the posture, initially for six breaths duration; then gradually increase the duration to a comfortable length of time.

Then slowly, bring the body down, one vertebra at a time, until the hip touches the floor; then bring the legs down to the floor.

From the sarvangasana position, flexing the hip and moving the legs to the back will help to facilitate lowering one vertebra at a time. Similarly, tilting the head back, also will help; however it is not advisable to raise the head, while lowering the vertebrae and the legs down. Then straighten the head back to the floor.

This completes the Sarvangasana.

7) THE FISH POSE– MATSYASANA

MATSYASANA always follows the Sarvangasana, in order to extend the spine that was flexed, during the Sarvangasana. Matsya in Sanskrit means fish.

Lie down flat on the floor facing up; and make a tight fist with both hands.
Place the fists under the sitting-bones aka ischial tuberosity.
Extend the cervical spine at the neck, by tilting the head backwards.
Now extend the remaining spine slowly, by raising the back upwards, away from the floor.
Then bring the legs to 'Ardha Padmasana', by flexing the legs at the knees and bringing the right foot

over the left thigh; or alternately, bring the legs to Sukhasana', the easy sitting pose.

Remain in this position for 6 breaths duration.

Then release the posture by un-tilting the head and placing the head on the floor; and take the fists away from the sitting bones, placing the back and hip on the floor.

Remain in the position and relax for about 3 to 6 breaths for the effect from the two powerful asanas to take place in the body.

8) THE BRIDGE POSE
SETU-BANDHA SARVANGASANA

HELPS TENNIS SERVE AND OVERHEAD

The bridge pose is another pose to extend the spine, similar to MATSYASANA.

Lie down flat and bend the knees up and at the same time, using the hands pull the heels of the feet close to the seat.

Extend the neck by tilting the head up.

Lift the back up and using the hands, support the back, extending the spine.

Note the chin is touching the chest, and knees should be together.

After about six breaths, release the pose, by removing the hand from the back and placing the spine on the floor slowly, one vertebra at a time. Then lie flat for some time, to allow the body to enjoy the effects of the pose. It is a good idea to lie down quietly for some time after each set of poses, described, for the same reason.

9) THE PLOUGH POSE — HALAASANA

HELPS TENNIS SAME WAY AS SARVANGASANA

It is appropriate to describe this Asana here, because the method of doing this pose is made simpler, by going into SARVANGASANA, as described above; then moving the legs all the way back until the legs touch the floor, above the head.

In the initial period, the legs may not reach the floor and that is understandable for a beginner or for someone with hip problem. With continuing practice, the legs will eventually touch the floor, above the head.

Hold the pose for about six breaths and increase the duration gradually to a comfortable duration.

Then release the pose by raising the feet up and lowering the back, one vertebra at a time, as described under Sarvangasana. Tilting the head back slightly–but not raising the head– will help to lower the back slowly.

10) MODIFIED SHOULDER STAND
VIPAREETA KARANI

IMPROVES CORE STRENGTH FOR TENNIS, INCREASING BLOOD SUPPLY TO PELVIS

Vipareeta Karani may seem like a variation of the Sarvangasana at the outset.

However, Vipareeta Karani is an important asana by itself, especially as one of the asanas recommended to raise the Kundalini Shakti. This asana increases the blood supply to the pelvic organs, thus strengthening the nerve supply also.

Similar to Sarvangasana, lie down flat and raise the legs and the hip, by pushing the palms and fingers against the floor.

Then hold the hip up by supporting the hip-bones in the back with thumbs and fingers.

The chin is not pressing on the sternum (unlike the Sarvangasana in which the chin presses on the chest).

Start by holding the pose for 6 breaths and gradually increase the duration.

Release the posture by lowering the hip and legs slowly.

Unlike Sarvangasana, the upper back remains on the floor in Vipareeta Karani.

11) BACK STRETCHING POSE PASCHIMOTTANASANA

IMPROVES CORE STRENGTH FOR TENNIS

Sit on the floor with the legs stretched out in front, and hands on knees.

Relaxing the back muscles, stretch the arms up, above the head, inhaling.

Exhaling, bend forwards from the hip and try to catch the big toes with the fingers; if this is not possible, hold the ankles with the hands. keep the neck extended, with the face looking forwards.

Breathe in and out normally.

Bending the elbows and placing them on either side of the legs, slowly bring the trunk down towards the thighs and the head towards the knees as much as possible.

Alternately, instead of raising the arms up in the beginning of this pose, slide the hands down from the knees to the toes or ankles.

Stay in the position, for as long as is comfortable.

Return to the sitting position.

Repeat 3 to 5 rounds.

DYNAMIC BACK STRETCH POSE–GATYATMAK PASCHIMOTTANASANA

IMPROVES CORE STRENGTH AND FLEXIBILITY FOR TENNIS

Start by lying flat on the back, with the arms stretched up above the head.

Relaxing the whole body, raise the trunk up, with the arms above the head.

Slowly bend forwards, as in PASCHIMOTTANASANA and stay in this position for a few seconds. Return to the sitting position and then the starting position, lying flat on the back, with the arms stretched up above the head, slowly.

This is one round.

Repeat 5 to 10 rounds.

Breathe in, coming to a sitting position.

Breathe out, bending forwards.

This is a dynamic asana that makes the whole body flexible and improves metabolism.

12) PIGEON POSE
EKA-PADA RAJAKAPOTANASANA

HELPS TO PREVENT LOW BACK PAIN AND SCIATICA PAIN

Eka Pada Raja Kapotasana helps to relieve sciatica pain. It is not uncommon to develop such pain in any sports activity as well as in daily activities.

There is a pair of muscles, called the Piriformis muscle, in the low back, situated deep in the pelvis, one on each side forming a pyramid. It is one of the lateral rotators of the hip. It arises from the anterior part of the sacrum mainly, and also from the sacroiliac joint capsule and sacro-tuberous ligament. It then travels through the greater sciatic foramen and attaches to the greater trochanter of the femur.

When it travels through the greater sciatic foramen, it divides the foramen into superior and inferior compartments. The superior gluteal nerve and vessels emerge superior to the piriformis muscle. The inferior gluteal nerve and vessels, along with the Sciatic nerve, travel inferior to the piriformis muscle.

Piriformis syndrome: In 17 percent of the population, the sciatic nerve pierces through the piriformis muscle. In such a person or in a person whose piriformis muscles are sprained or strained, the sciatic nerve that runs adjoining the muscles may be pinched;

and sciatica pain can occur.

Sciatica presents as pain deep in the pelvis, inside the buttocks, along with tingling or numbness; the pain also may travel along the course of the sciatic nerve in the back of the thigh. The sciatica pain may increase with sitting, squatting or climbing stairs.

The pain from a slipped disc has a different location in the back; however, a slipped disc and problems of the spine need to be ruled out by a physician, using MRI and X-rays.

Pigeon pose or Eka Pada RajaKapotasana is known to relieve the sciatica pain of piriformis syndrome.

Start from the 'Parvatasana'– the downward facing dog pose; bring the right leg forwards, bending the right knee and placing the shin close to the hands on the floor, as parallel as possible to the hands, preferably between the hands.
Place the dorsal or top part of the left foot on the floor and look up, stretching the trunk. Now lower the perineum or pelvic diaphragm down towards the floor, as much as possible. Placing the left foot on its toes will help this step. One may also bring the elbows to the floor, placing the palms on the floor, in front.

Stay in this pose for 6 breaths and gradually increase the duration to a comfortable level.

Reverse the steps to return to the PARVATASANA– the downward facing dog– and repeat on the other side.

Reverse the steps again and return to the standing PRANAMASANA pose.

THE RELAXING POSE– SAVAASANA

HELPS TO REDUCE TIGHTNESS DURING THE GAME OF TENNIS.

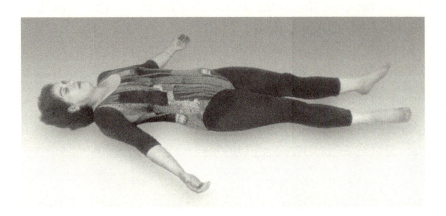

TECHNIQUE DURING THE GAME OF TENNIS:

The Savasana method can also be used during the game, if you find yourself tightening up and making unforced errors. (Please do not lie down in the middle of the tennis court to do the Savasana!) When you feel the need to loosen the body, during the game, simply bend your knees; tighten both the leg muscles and let go the tightness gradually, similar to the Savasana method, described below. Then tighten both arms with clenched fist and let go the tightness gradually. Observe your normal breathing

SAVASANA METHOD:

Lie down flat on the back; raise one leg slightly, contract the leg muscles and drop the leg to the floor. Repeat the same for the other leg.

Raise and contract and drop one arm at a time.

Contract the neck muscles and relax; move the head to one side, then the other side and bring it to the middle, three times.

Contract all the facial muscles and let go.

Raise the shoulders up towards the ears and back; and then drop the shoulders down and place the shoulders on the floor

Repeat the above steps, if needed for the relaxing process.

Breathe normally and notice your breathing, slowing down without effort.

Thus, relaxing the whole body, lie down with eyes gently closed for a few minutes, as time permits.

Then turn the body to one side, and supporting yourself with your palm on the floor, slowly get up; stand with the feet at hip width and palms together at chest level, close your eyes and chant Aum slowly three times. This concludes the Yoga-asana practices.

4. MIND MECHANICS

THE MENTAL GAME
LOVE ALL

Tennis is one of the games that start with a score of Love-All. This wonderful attitude, however, may get mangled and disturbed sometimes, due to reactions of the mind, such as anger and anxiety during the play.

In the game of Tennis, besides the use of the body and the racquet, mind plays a significant role. For example, in both recreational and competitive tennis, one of the players loses a point and loses the mind and acts irrationally, throwing the racquet or kicking something with rage. Then, it begins to affect the game as well. What is needed here is anger control; but unfortunately, anger management cannot be done at the tennis court. It has to start with management of the mind in general, outside the tennis court.

MIND YOUR MIND

Mind is one of the functions of the body. The mind is the functional aspect of the brain. If brain is understood as the hardware, the mind can be considered as the software of a computer. However, the psycho-neuro-endocrine system along with *hormones, neurotransmitters and enzymes,* with their compensatory feed-back mechanism differentiate the mind and body from a computer. Similarly, the *Limbic system* responsible for emotions also distinguish the mind and body from a super computer.

We manage the body with exercise, yoga, sports and other activities. Similarly, we need to manage the mind. Now understanding the mind itself is important for the purpose of mind management, including anger management, anxiety management and general well-being. So, mind mechanics including the mind and brain and how they function as a part of the body will be described here in detail in this chapter.

Mind can be a friend or enemy. As an enemy, it can bring about anger, anxiety, arrogance, jealousy, fear or depression. As a friend, mind can bring balance to life and can be a guiding light. Understanding the mind gives *clarity* and will keep the mind as a friend and guide; and provide health and happiness in life.

So, a brief explanation of how the brain and the mind work, as applicable to our present discussion of mind-mechanics and mind management, is given below.

THE HUMAN BRAIN

The human brain contains over one hundred billion nerve cells, known as neurons that communicate with connections, known as synapses which number in trillions. Even though the human brain has the same structures as that of other mammals, it is relatively larger in size. It is also much more specialized and unique in the cerebral cortex with higher reasoning capacity and is able to learn and speak languages. The brain consists of

1. the cerebrum
2. the cerebellum
3. the brain stem

THE CEREBRAL CORTEX

The cerebrum has the cerebral cortex as the outermost layer of the cerebrum and consists of four lobes on each side. The cerebral cortex has multiple deep folds, known as gyrus(gyri) and sulcus(sulci), thus increasing the surface area many fold. The lobes of the cerebral cortex are

1. The frontal lobe
2. The parietal lobe
3. The temporal lobe and
4. The occipital lobe

For a right- handed person, the functions of the right side of the body are controlled by the left side of the brain and the left side of the body are controlled by the right side of the brain.

The frontal lobe is situated in the front of the brain, as the name implies; and is responsible for the functions of reasoning, language, higher level of cognition and motor skills. The motor cortex is located at the back of the frontal lobe and provides voluntary movements as needed.

The parietal lobe is situated behind the frontal lobe and lodges the somatosensory-cortex which is responsible for the processing of the senses, such as touch, pain and pressure.

The temporal lobe is in the lower section of the brain and contains the auditory cortex that is needed for hearing. The hippocampus, a part of the limbic system is situated in the temporal lobe and is responsible for the function of *memories*.

The occipital lobe is in the back portion of the brain and contains the visual cortex that is essential for seeing and receives information from the retinas that form the back of the eyes. The right sides of both retinae are controlled by the left visual cortex; and the left sides of both retinae are controlled by the right visual cortex.

THE CEREBELLUM

The cerebellum is situated behind the brain stem and below the cerebrum.

Even though it is relatively smaller in size, it contains more than 50 percent of the total neurons of the brain, i.e., over fifty billion neurons. It helps to control posture, balance and the coordination of voluntary movements.

THE BRAIN STEM
The brain stem consists of
1. hindbrain and
2. midbrain.

1. The hindbrain consists of medulla, reticular formation and pons.
The *medulla* or medulla oblongata connects the brain to the spinal cord and controls the autonomic functions, heart rate, blood pressure and breathing.

The *reticular formation* is a network of nerves in the medulla and helps to control functions of sleep and attention.

The *pons* is located between the medulla and cerebrum and helps to coordinate movement on each side of the body.

2. The Midbrain is the smallest structure of the brain. The midbrain contains a cluster of structures called the *basal ganglia.*
It coordinates messages between multiple areas of the brain. It controls visual and auditory systems as well as eye movement.
The part of the midbrain that contains *substantia nigra* and *red nucleus* control the body movement. The substantia nigra contains a large number of dopamine

producing neurons; the degeneration of these neurons causes Parkinson's disease.

THE MIND

The mind is the functional aspect of the brain and collects data from its surroundings, by way of the five senses and the corresponding sense organs of ears, skin, eyes, tongue and nose.

The *Thalamus* acts as a relay station, receiving messages from all the sensory receptors of the body and sending the information to the different regions of the brain, as described earlier. These data are either used in the present moment or stored in the memory as past events. The mind also is able to analyze the data and come to conclusions.

THE LIMBIC SYSTEM AND EMOTIONS

The emotional aspect of the mind functions through the limbic system of the brain. The limbic system includes various structures, such as *hippocampus, amygdala, limbic cortex and the septal area* which form connections to the hypothalamus, thalamus and cerebral cortex.

These structures are involved in emotions, learning and memory. The Limbic system operates by influencing

1. The endocrine system and
2. The autonomic nervous system.

It acts on the endocrine system through the

hypothalamus, which regulates all the endocrine glands by way of various releasing factors, which regulate the various *trophic hormones from the pituitary gland;*

e. g., thyrotrophin-releasing-factor from the hypothalamus regulates the thyrotrophin secretion from the pituitary gland; which in turn regulates the thyroid hormones from the thyroid gland.

Similarly, various trophic (stimulating) hormones are secreted by the pituitary gland, such as *adrenocorticotrophic hormone* regulating *cortisol* from the adrenal cortex, and *gonadotrophin hormone* that acts on ovaries and testes, etc. The pituitary gland is therefore aptly called the *master of the orchestra.*

Oxytocin, another hormone produced in the hypothalamus and stored in the posterior pituitary gland is given a nick-name of 'love-hormone' or bonding hormone. Recent studies associate this hormone in various bonding relationships in both men and women, such as orgasm and especially in women both during and after childbirth. Supposedly, it is released in large amounts in child birth during the dilation of the uterine cervix; and helping the labor and promoting maternal bonding and lactation after child birth. This hormone is also used during childbirth as a 'Pitocin-drip', for uterine contraction, if needed.

The other hormone from the posterior pituitary is

called Vasopressin or Anti-diuretic hormone (ADH). As the name implies, it causes an increase in blood pressure, by water retention and contraction of arterioles. Reduced secretion of ADH causes Diabetes Insipidus, by acting on the tubules of the kidneys to produce excessive dilute urine, which results in dehydration. Male aggression is reported to be associated with this hormone.

The limbic system also influences the autonomic nervous system which consists of the sympathetic system and the para-sympathetic system.
Epinephrine and nor-epinephrine are the hormones of the sympathetic system, secreted by the adrenal medulla. *Acetyl-choline* is the hormone of the para-sympathetic system.

ANGER AND SYMPATHETIC SYSTEM

Anger is a reaction to a situation either self-created or created by others. Anger expresses itself through the sympathetic system by secreting more adrenaline from adrenal medulla and sympathetic nerve endings; and by secreting more cortisol from adrenal cortex.

Anger and its association with the adrenaline response, leading to increased heart rate and stress response with increased cortisol are well documented.

Whatever situation or person is the source of the anger, the person 'reacting' with anger is the only one who can manage the 'reaction', i.e., by 'acting' instead of reacting to the situation. The method of management is further explained under 'anger management'.

Parasympathetic stimulation, in general, causes relaxation and lessening of anxiety. This is made use of in many of the yoga poses and pranayama breathing that stimulate the *Vagus* nerve. The Vagus is one of the cranial nerves (tenth cranial nerve). It is named the vagus nerve, because it takes a meandering and long course all over, like a vagabond from the brain all the way down to the abdomen, giving out multiple branches along the way in the head, neck, thorax and abdomen. Besides its motor and sensory functions, it is a parasympathetic nerve and thus helps in lowering anxiety and improving relaxation of the mind.

NEUROTRANSMITTERS

Neurotransmitters are chemicals that transmit messages across the synapses of neurons (the nerve cells). The human body consists of about 100 billion neurons. Some of the important neurotransmitters are Epinephrine, Acetylcholine, Cortisol, Dopamine, Melatonin, Serotonin, GABA–gamma amino butyric acid– and Endorphin.

Thus, the various structures of the Limbic system, with varying degrees of emotional attachment and memory of past events, form a part of the network of the psycho-neuro-endocrine system.

MEMORY AND ANGER

The limbic system, briefly explained above, is involved in Emotions, such as anger; and also in memory. The Cerebral Cortex also plays a part in memory. The past events are stored in the brain as memory. Very often, these stored *past* events from memory are the trigger for anger in a person.

Future planning of a successful outcome or ambition along with *emotional attachment* also can be a trigger for the onset of anger. For example, in the game of tennis, with a game score of 6-6 and a 'tie-breaker' score of 6-5, the serving player is unable to hold the point to win the set-point for a successful outcome and eventually loses the game and/or the match; and this failure of the planned successful outcome can be a trigger, depending on the degree of *emotional attachment* in that situation.

The mind and body are not independent of each other and can be considered as one entity. For example, the brain is an anatomical part of the body and the mind is one of the physiological functions of the brain.

The brain, as alluded to earlier, contains over one hundred billion neurons which are all connected with trillions of synapses which send messages.

Recent studies also reveal that the neurons produce

many hormone-like neurotransmitters, such as dopamine, serotonin, endorphin and gamma-amino-butyric acid (GABA) that influence the mind. It makes us wonder if the brain can be a very large and complex endocrine gland; on the other hand, if all the endocrine glands with their hormones, can be considered part of the brain.

When the mind goes into anger mode, the body reacts with increased secretion of adrenaline hormone (aka epinephrine) from the medulla part of the adrenal glands, similar to *fight or flight* response or survival response.

This increases the pulse rate and blood pressure; the eyes become red.

Similarly, the mind reacts to the occurrences of the body.

For example, if the finger goes near fire accidentally, there is pain--the sensory nerves take the message from the affected finger to the brain, to the area of touch, pain and temperature; and the brain reacts instantly and sends the message through the motor nerves to the corresponding arm muscles to pull back the hand quickly. All of these happen in a split second. In fact, the pain is a warning sign, given by the anatomical brain to the finger, through the physiological pain sensation. The nerve to the brain is a sensory nerve and the nerve from the brain to the arm muscles is considered as a motor nerve.

If the fire happens to be severe, resulting in burns to the area, the emotional part of the mind also comes into play and shows further disappointment and anger. If the fire was caused by another person, then the mind may react with anger towards that person.

Similarly, when there is '*itis*' or inflammation of any part of the body, e.g., appendicitis, there is pain which is a warning sign. But if it is not treated properly, the mind may show anger and disappointment.

DEPRESSION AFTER HEART ATTACK

Another example where the mind reacts to the ailment of the body, is heart attack. Even after the proper treatment of the cardiac episode, presenting with severe pain, it is not uncommon for the patient to go into *depression,* with feelings of self-pity and the mind questioning why 'IT' had to happen to him. Besides depression, *insomnia* also is a common occurrence, after heart attack, needing sleeping pill for adequate rest.

EGO

Past events along with future plans and ambitions give the mind one's personality or ego. Thus, the personality is a combination of the past and future; and not the present moment of awareness. This is how the anger episodes are the result of and a part of one's personality; and not a reflection of the *Awareness of the present moment.* Here again, the emphasis should be on

Awareness and not in the *present moment*.

PROBLEM WITH PRESENT MOMENT

Many of the teachings that stress upon the *present moment* have failed because of the misguided emphasis on the *present moment,* instead of on *Awareness. Present moment* is *time based,* because the present moment is as opposed to *past and future* and will always be controlled by the *mind*; whereas *Awareness is beyond mind* and is not limited by the problems of mind. That is the reason many of the teachings that emphasize on present moment have failed. This Awareness is more evident in the higher intelligence of human beings, because the higher intelligence of human beings is capable of *being Aware.* Thus, human beings do not have to react on instinct, with anger that is part of the mind, for example, like animals. The *Awareness* will be further explained in detail below.

AWARENESS AND MIND

Human beings are intelligent enough to be aware of one's own thoughts. The word, "thought" itself is the past tense of the word, "think". So, most of the thoughts are of past events or past thinking. Awareness has the capacity to be aware of all things that are based in time and space, especially in the present moment. Thoughts are *time-based* and pertain to the past. Thus, Awareness provides the capacity to be aware of *one's own thoughts*, as and when they occur; in other words, to be aware of the mind itself.

Awareness is also called consciousness sometimes, creating confusion because consciousness generally pertains to consciousness of the mind as opposed to unconsciousness; whereas Awareness, in this context, pertains to being aware of the mind itself. That is the reason the word, Awareness is being used here, instead of the word, consciousness.

5. MIND MANAGEMENT

LIFE-ENERGY AND MUTUALLY INHERENT AWARENESS

In one of the two great Epics of India, Mahabharata [the other being Ramayana], King Yudishtara, the eldest brother of the five Pandavas in exile was asked many questions by a lake-demon, after his four younger brothers swooned on drinking the lake water. The King answered them correctly and saved his brothers. One of the questions was "what is the most surprising thing in the world?" The King answered; "people see others dying and taken to the funeral pyre every day and yet they think they will live forever." The demon was satisfied with that answer.

Similar to the concept above, we see babies born all the time and people passing away every day; yet we take the *Life Energy Principle or the Life Force*— that *appears* to come and go with the body— for granted. In fact, it is the body that comes and goes within the *Life-Force or Life Energy.* We ignore the most *fundamental* of this very existence. We also ignore *'Awareness',* that is *inherent* in the Life Energy, even though we are aware of the Awareness. Instead, we confuse this *Limitless Awareness* with the limited consciousness and sub-consciousness, that are part of the mind. The mind is very clever; and like a Chameleon changing colors, the mind, *limited* by nature, puts on the color of consciousness or awareness and claims ownership of the Awareness that is in fact *limitless and all-pervasive and Beyond Mind.* How can the mind, limited by nature contain *Awareness* that is limitless and all-pervasive along with the Life Force or Life-Energy.

PROOF OF AWARENESS BEING BEYOND MIND

Awareness is always *Universal and Limitless.* Mind is always individualized and limited, even when it expresses the Awareness and is *Aware.* But mind cannot contain the Limitless Awareness and cannot be the source of the Universal Awareness

That is proven by the example, given below when a person is in *deep sleep or* has a *fainting episode,* losing consciousness of the mind. Here again, notice that the mind is losing the consciousness and *turned off* similar to a computer being turned off. Again, the Awareness with its *Inherent Life-Energy* that always *exists,* that is the source of everything including the mind, does not become *non-existent* in those instances of fainting or deep sleep.

Even though the mind is used as an instrument in the understanding of Awareness, the limitless Awareness cannot be contained in the limited mind. The mind is similar to a stick that is used to kindle a camp-fire which consumes the stick; and the camp-fire remains. Sri Ramakrishna, a *Mystic* who lived in the 19th century compared the mind to the stick that is used to kindle the *funeral* pyre; and the stick i.e., the mind is consumed in the fire and the fire remains, representing the realization of *Self,* the ultimate goal of Vedanta philosophy.

The mind can be contained in the Awareness; i.e., the Awareness can be aware of the mind, as a flow of thoughts. But Awareness exists even when the mind is turned off, as in deep sleep.

If we close the eyes and pick up a cup with the hand, we realize that act; i.e., we are aware of the function of the hand, through the senses. By closing the eyes, the seeing-sense is removed; but the tactile sense of the finger, touching the cup is present. However, in a person with an artificial arm, for example, the tactile sense and the motor function are removed. So, the sense and the part of the brain that collects the sensory data, are not likely to be aware of the act of picking up the cup. Perhaps here, the higher intelligence that can be aware of the functioning of the mind and a part of the function of the mind to activate the artificial limb are what are behind the awareness of the act of picking up the cup.

Let us take another example. When we are asleep

or during fainting spells, the mind is turned off and in those moments, we have no *identity* and we do not know where we are, not unlike putting the computer to sleep-mode. Even though the mind is asleep, in *deep-sleep and during fainting spells,* the essential functions of the body, such as cardio-vascular system, respiratory system and the hormonal system keep the body functioning and alive due to the existence of *Life-Energy and the Inherent Awareness.*

This Life-Energy along with the Inherent Awareness keeps the brain and the mind alive, along with memory and along with the data of who we are, even though the mind is completely turned off, in deep sleep and during fainting spells. However, when we wake up, the mind becomes alive and awake; and has no question about our identity and proceeds with regular functioning of the body and mind.

The Mind itself is not unlike a super-computer. A computer has hardware and software and the data are stored and maintained by the computer's energy. Our mind has hardware: the brain; and software: the mind. However, the addition of Limbic system that is responsible for the *emotions* and the *psycho-neuro-endocrine system with feed-back mechanism* that is responsible for the maintenance of the *Internal Milieu* distinguish the mind and brain from a supercomputer.

Brain, the hardware, as described earlier, has the

cerebral cortex, cerebellum, brain stem with the midbrain along with the multiple structures of hippocampus, amygdala, thalamus and the hypothalamus together called the limbic system, connecting to an elaborate network of 100 billion neurons, through neurotransmitters and hormones.

The mind, the software, functions with analytical, logical and creative capabilities with sensory receptors and motor functions; and through the limbic system, is the seat of emotions, learning and memory.

BOSONS

In the macrocosm as well as the microcosm, there are energy particles known as electrons, everywhere, and these subatomic particles form the basic unit and manifest as billions of galaxies. There are also subatomic particles, even smaller than the electrons, known as Bosons, considered now as the basic unit of *All Matter*.

The recent discovery of Higgs Particles, known as Bosons, by the Nobel Laureates, Peter Higgs of the University of Edinburgh in Scotland and Francois Englert of the University Libre de Bruxelles, further clarifies the understanding of the subatomic particles as the basic unit of all matter.

THE THEORY OF MUTUALLY INHERENT LIFE-ENERGY AND AWARENESS-INTELLIGENCE

It is mind-boggling to comprehend how subatomic particles, described as the Higgs-Boson particle above, along with the Forces of Nature– Gravity, Electromagnetism, Weak Nuclear Force and Strong Nuclear Force–manifest as billions of galaxies and how all *matter* appears, disappears and reappears constantly. It is perfectly reasonable to infer that the immensity and precision of the workings of the *cosmos* can only function and exist with a high degree of intelligence.

For every action, some degree of intelligence is needed to provide the knowledge of the act. So, such intelligence has to be present in the structural and functional agency that initiates the action.

Similarly, the *energy particles forming all matter* have to have an *Inherent Intelligence* to provide the knowledge to form matter.

I call this Intelligence as the *Inherent-Awareness-Intelligence*; and the energy particles as the *Life-Energy* that is all-pervasive. This Awareness-Intelligence is inherent in the all-pervasive Life-Energy; and this all-pervasive Life-Energy is inherent in its Awareness-Intelligence. So, they are both mutually inherent and inseparable from each other. I call this 'the mutual inherence of the Life-Energy and Awareness'.

It is beyond the scope of this discussion on tennis and yoga to delve into any theoretical physics or theological questions that may arise, as a result of this theory. The reader is referred to *other books by this author*, on this subject.

This Inherent-Awareness-Intelligence is present as the substratum, in the world we live in, as well as in the cosmos with the precise functioning of planets and stars and billions of galaxies and multiple universes, in spite of any *chaos in the cosmos as well as in the human mind.*

What is unique for human beings is that the higher Intelligence of humans is capable of being aware of this Awareness. The higher Awareness-Intelligence of humans is also capable of being aware of the mind itself.

This Life-Energy with Inherent Awareness is *all-pervasive*: I call this 'the *Theory of Mutually Inherent Life-Energy and Awareness-Intelligence'*.

THE TECHNIQUE OF ANGER MANAGEMENT

In the technique of anger management, the above described Awareness can be effectively used as follows:

This awareness capability of the human intelligence can also see one's own mind as thoughts. Just like we can see the hand with our eyes, we can learn to see our own thoughts; i.e., to be aware of the thought. So the technique is to see the thoughts-- in other words, to be aware of the thoughts --as and when the thoughts occur during the day. This technique of seeing the thoughts has to be developed as a *habit*, during the normal activities of the day, when there is no anger.

To further elucidate, human beings have the capacity to realize this Awareness; i.e., to be aware of the Awareness. Developmentally, human beings are at a more mature level than animals to be aware of this Awareness, whereas animals have the capacity to think and act on instinct only. That is the difference between human beings and animals.

So, when men or women act on instinct only, the animal nature predominates. On the other hand, when men or women act with *kindness and good Intentions*, the Divine nature predominates.
Animals also have the Divine nature of Kindness and Good intentions, in varying degrees. We have all seen pet dogs that are tolerant and kind to children, even when they sit on the back of the dog.

Humans, however, have a higher intelligence and the ability to be aware of the flow of thoughts and the ability to choose. The well- known psychologist, Carl Jung developed his system of 'psycho-analysis' based on this awareness-intelligence, also known as consciousness.

Human beings are a complex combination of animal nature and divine nature. In our daily life, we all have a predominance of either divine nature or animal nature. When the animal nature takes over, generally speaking, we react to circumstances, instinctively.

This results in outbursts of anger or feelings of jealousy or attitudes of arrogance or vanity or greed. All of these have a common thread of *reacting instinctively* to the circumstances; and anger tops them all because the outbursts of anger are uncontrollable for that person, at that moment.

That is the reason this technique of seeing thoughts is recommended and then the person can be Aware of thoughts as they occur and then it becomes a habit in due course. However, trying to be aware of the reaction of anger only at the time of anger is not possible, unless one cultivates a habit of seeing the reactions of one's own mind, as they occur, in less severe circumstances. Cultivation of this habit is the key to anger management, not only on the tennis court but, *in daily life as well.*

STRESS MANAGEMENT

Hans Selye introduced the term *Stress* in the twentieth century and proved that the hormone cortisol, from the adrenal cortex, is increased at times of stress.

Stress is a part of life and cannot be totally

avoided. After one accepts the inevitability of stressful situations coming and going, one has to learn how to cope with stress; therein lies the prevention of damage to our mind and life.

People often say that a person externalizes his or her reaction to stress by acting out one's emotions of frustration and/or anger. In the same way, we say that a person internalizes his or her reactions to various situations, if one does not show the emotions outside.

Most people wrongly assume that externalizing a stress reaction is better, because the common concept is that internalization leads to suppression of emotions in the subconscious mind, causing inevitable damage to the psyche, resulting in damage to the body as well; and at some future time, the welled-up emotions might burst out.

The truth is, the above described internalization and the externalization concepts pertain to the emotional and mental make-up of reactions of the mind in general. So both of them cause equal amount of damage to the mind and body of that person, not to mention the ramifications involved in various relationships in different situations of stress.

So, the internalization and externalization of reactions to stress do not appear to be the proper approach to managing stress.

Then what is the proper approach to stress management? First of all, one needs to comprehend and view internalization and externalization as products of the mind and its reactions; they both need to be viewed as external; and together they are to be viewed as a mental response.

In order to successfully manage stress, one has to take on a *Supra-mental approach.* In the supra-mental approach, one views the situation, as though from a gallery above, that is playing out the different roles of a drama; this way one can assess the situation quickly without reacting. Hence one will be able to come up with a solution for the immediate moment as well as for the long term.

Here again the body and mind are together viewed as an instrument- the body being the outer instrument and the mind being the inner instrument.

This technique of being aware of the mind have been dealt with in detail under 'Anger Management'. The reader is advised to refer to the same for further details.

ANXIETY MANAGEMENT

Anxiety, on the tennis court for example, expresses itself as choking; it often comes up when the player is winning, for example, by 5 games to 2 and the player has to get just one more game to win the match. When anxiety takes over, attention to playing the point is diverted to thoughts of winning the sixth game and finishing the set; this thought process keeps the anxiety level up and takes away attention from the ball and the movement of the body that are needed to execute shots.

So, the antidote is to pay attention again to each point, focusing on the ball and executing the necessary movement of the body and the racquet, which is like an extension of the body at that moment.

This is true in life also:
Let us examine the nature of anxiety in a little more depth; anxiety is usually about the future- namely, the result of the action that is taking place, the effect that is going to happen as a result of the action. On close scrutiny, we find that we only have control over what we are doing; not over the result thereof. This has been analyzed and explained in Bhagavad Gita, an ancient text that explains how to perform our duty or any action in our daily life, without anxiety, as an advice given by Sri Krishna to Arjuna in the battlefield— metaphorically in the *battlefield of our mind*.

So, the technique to avoid anxiety is to *focus* on the action itself; and not on what is going to happen or what might happen; in other words, not on the results of the action that causes fear. Fear is the cause of anxiety.

Anxiety can also be triggered by recollection of past events in one's life.

Even though it is very obvious that past is dead, a person holds on to the past in his memory bank and the memory is brought back up, based on one's personality to establish itself. Again, on close scrutiny, we find that the personality exists as the compilation of past and future, namely the past events stored in the memory and future ambitions and wishes. In order to avoid letting past events and memories cloud the present, the technique, again, is to *focus* on the action itself, in the present moment. The emphasis here again is on the word, *focus*.

"Dead yesterday, Unborn tomorrow
Why fret about them,
If today be sweet?"

– Omar Khayyam, Sufi poet

6. PRANAYAMA

Hatha Yoga Pradipika, an ancient yoga text says that the mind is the king of the senses and Prana is the king of the mind. The function of the mind is to gather information through the senses; of hearing through the ears; of touch, pain and temperature through the skin; of seeing through the eyes; of taste though the tongue; and smell though the nose.

The mind also mediates speech, the motor functions of the upper and lower extremities, and the actions of excretion and procreation. Animals also use the mind to gather the above five senses and to perform the above five motor functions.

However, the intelligence to analyze, discuss and deliberate is of much higher caliber in human beings. Perhaps, for the same reason, humans have stronger egos.

Emotions also play a role in the functioning of the mind. The right side of the body is controlled by the left side of the brain and is called the dominant side-- for a right- handed person-- and vice versa.

Generally, the left side of the brain is responsible for analytical and logical thinking and the right brain is considered to be responsible for the creative and intuitive contributions of the mind. However, the right and left sides cross over in the middle of the brain.

As we discussed before, the mind, namely the flow of thoughts, can only be regulated by either approaching it from *below the level of the mind* through the different breathing techniques of Pranayama; or from *above the mind,* by paying attention to the mind and thus being aware of thoughts as and when they occur, a habit described in "Anger Management". This habit regulates the flow of thoughts and eventually remains beyond the problems of the mind, described earlier as the *supra-mental approach.*

PRANAYAMA:

Pranayama is helpful because the breathing is deliberate, and also helps in the control of mind. The different techniques of Pranayama are described below.

Before doing pranayama, traditionally, one should drink three sips of water.
There is an important reason behind this ritual, namely to prevent aspiration of food-particles that may be lodged in the throat.

YOGIC BREATHING– DEEP BREATHING

Yogic Breathing is a type of Pranayama and can be practiced at any time or place, and without much training or guidance.

The technique is as follows:
Inhalation:
There are three phases in the inhalation.
1. In the first phase of breathing in, the abdomen slightly pushes out, filling the lower, wider parts of the lungs.
2. In the second phase of inhalation, when the middle parts of the lungs are filled with air, the chest pushes out. When the chest expands, the abdomen tends to pull in; it is not advisable to keep the abdomen pushed out.
3. In the third phase, the collar bones go up, when the shoulders are pulled back and up, expanding the chest further, filling the apical or upper parts of the lungs

Exhalation:
For breathing out, the steps are reversed; namely the shoulders drop down; the chest and abdomen relax.

This type of deep breathing stimulates the *Vagus* nerve which is a parasympathetic nerve; thus, this technique brings about relaxation and reduces anxiety and lowers the heart rate.

PRANAYAMA METHODS
In the Pranayama method,
1. Puraka means breathing in.
2. Rechaka means breathing out.
3. Kumbhaka means retention.

This is generally done in the proportion of 1: 4: 2 for inhalation, retention, and exhalation, respectively. However, whenever Kumbakha or retention of breath is included in the practice, this is considered an advanced Pranayama and it is advisable to seek guidance from a teacher who is familiar with this method.

For beginners, the retention is to be started at 1: 1: 1 for inhalation, retention and exhalation; and one may slowly build the retention up to 4. So, the 1:4:2 ratio should not be practiced in the beginning; it should be 1:1:1, and gradually increased. This ratio of 1:4:2 is only mentioned here as the traditional system of practice.

Once you master the 1:1:1 ratio, you may start the 1:1:2 ratio using the proportion of 1:1:2 for inhalation, retention and exhalation. This will help to increase the duration and intensity of the next 'breathing-in'. To reiterate this point, the exhalation should be done 'slowly' and be longer in duration.

The practice of Pranayama, if one wants to pursue it, should be done carefully and slowly and gradually increased as follows:

Sit comfortably in ArdhaPadmasana (half-lotus pose) or Vajrasana (legs folded back and sitting on the heels of the feet) or Sukhasana (comfortable sitting position) or in a chair, if it is preferred. Use the right hand for closing and opening the nostrils; the thumb for the right nostril and the ring and little fingers for the left nostril.

1. IPSI-LATERAL OR SAME-SIDE PRANAYAMA

Inhalation through the Left nostril
Exhalation through the same nostril
Repeat 6 times; start with 3 times and gradually increase to 6 times.
There is no Retention in this Pranayama.
Repeat the above steps through the Right nostril.

2. BILATERAL OR BOTH SIDES PRANAYAMA

Inhalation through both nostrils
Exhalation through both nostrils, slowly.
Repeat 6 times; start with 3 times and gradually increase to 6 times.
There is no retention in this Pranayama
This is similar to 'Yogic Breathing'.

3. CONTRALATERAL OR ALTERNATE SIDES PRANAYAMA

This is also known as 'Nadi Sodhana'.
Inhalation through the Left nostril
Exhalation through the Right nostril
Inhalation through the same --Right-- nostril
Exhalation through the Left nostril
This is one cycle.
Repeat 3 times and gradually increase to 6 times

4. ALTERNATE SIDES---NADI SODHANA PRANAYAMA WITH KUMBHAKA

As mentioned above, this advanced system should be done with guidance from a Yoga teacher.

In the Nadi Sodhana type of Pranayama, one inhales for one count through the left nostril and holds for one count and then the exhales through the right nostril for twice as long–so the proportion between Puraka and Kumbhaka and Rechaka– inhalation and retention and exhalation, is as follows:

1:1:2.

One can use either the number or the word "OM." Then the duration is increased gradually, taking care to use the same proportion;

1:1:2
2:2:4
3:3:6
4:4:8 and so on
The method is as follows:
Inhalation through the left nostril.

Retention.
Exhalation through the right nostril.
Inhalation through the right nostril.
Retention.
Exhalation through the left nostril.

This completes one cycle. This is the Puraka-Kumbhaka type of Nadi Sodhana.

KUMBHAKA

In the Kumbhaka or retention phase, the chin-lock or *Jalandhara Bandha* and rectal contraction or *Moola-Bandha* are recommended to be done in that order; and at the end of retention, rectal contraction is relaxed first and then the chin-lock is released, before the exhalation.

The chin-lock is done by bringing the chin to the top of the sternum (the breast bone), with slight flexion of the neck.

After a month of this practice, one may do Rechaka-Kumbhaka as follows:
Inhalation through the left nostril.
Exhalation through the right nostril.
Retention.
Inhalation through the right nostril.
Exhalation through the left nostril.
Retention.

The proportion for the above is 1:1:1 in the

beginning. After a month of this practice, the proportion can be increased gradually to 1: 2: 4 for inhalation, exhalation, and retention respectively, as follows:
1:1:1
1:2:2
1:2:3
1:2:4

It is very important not to increase the proportion prematurely; in fact it is not important to do any of these methods vigorously and it is more important to do them consistently every day and preferably at the same time of the day.

Next, the above two, namely Purakha-Kumbakha and Rechaka-Kumbakha, i.e., inhalation-retention and exhalation-retention can be combined as follows:
Inhalation
Retention
Exhalation
Retention
Inhalation
Retention
Exhalation,
using the gradual progression ratio, as mentioned above.
So, the point is to progress gradually in Pranayama.

A WORD OF CAUTION.

A word of caution is warranted here regarding the retention phase of pranayama. Retention is not advised for anyone with health problems, such as high blood-pressure, cardiac or pulmonary diseases.

If you are starting the practice in the later years of life, retention is not advised. In fact, for any age, a moment of retention both after inhalation and after exhalation is all that is needed; and it is strongly recommended that any pranayama practice that includes retention or Kumbhaka should be done under the guidance of a yoga teacher who is familiar with pranayama .

SPECIALIZED PRANAYAMAS

Besides the regular Pranayama described above, there are some specialized Pranayama practices that are recommended with some specific benefits. For example, *Bastrika or bellow-breathing* increases the heat in the body and so it is advisable to practice Bastrika more in the winter season and less in the summer.

Seethali tends to cool the body and so it is beneficial generally in the summer season. However, it also helps to lower blood pressure in patients with high blood pressure; hence, it can be practiced regularly in such circumstances.

It is advisable to seek guidance in learning these techniques.

BASTRIKA OR BELLOW BREATHING

As mentioned above, Bastrika increases the heat in the body; it also increases the energy in the body and so morning time is best suited for practice of this breathing. It is best not to do Bastrika before bed-time, to avoid sleep disturbances. It is also preferable to have empty stomach or three hours after a meal or at least one hour after drinking any liquid.

One sits comfortably on the floor or in a chair without arms (to avoid restriction of the elbows, when the arms are placed on the knees).

Place the hands firmly on the knees and take a deep breath in and out; and start the bellow like movement of the abdominal muscles, breathing out when the abdomen is pulled in; and breathing in when the abdomen is pushed out.

The emphasis is on breathing out and pulling the abdomen in. The breathing in and out are of equal proportion and are done with both nostrils.

Start at a comfortable pace and increase the pace faster to about 20 times; then take a take a deep breath in and slowly breath out, pulling the abdomen in, to complete one cycle. Repeat 3 to 6 times as needed.

Besides increasing body heat as mentioned above, it also helps to prevent allergy symptoms, perhaps by regulating the adrenal hormones. The adrenal glands are situated in the back of the abdominal cavity, above the kidneys. So, the Bastrika is also advised in the spring season or allergy season, when the pollen count is high, to prevent nasal allergy symptoms.

KAPAALA BHATI

Kapala means the head or skull in Sanskrit; bhati means 'shines'. Kapaala-bhati helps one to have a shining face.

It also helps one to prevent nasal allergy symptoms. The method is similar to Bastrika; the main difference is that in Kapaala Bhati, the abdomen is used minimally, and the forceful expirations happen at the nose level in Kapaala Bhati.

Sit comfortably on the floor or in a chair. Similar to Bastrika, the method is to do forceful exhalations about 20 times rapidly; and then take a deep breath in and slowly breathe out. The rapid exhalations are similar to blowing the nose to clear the nasal passages; the exhalations are done with both nostrils. There is only a slight movement of the abdomen with each rapid exhalation.

VIPAREETA SVASA.

The method is similar to the above KapaalaBhati, except the rapid exhalation-movements are done at the tip of the nose.

Pulling the tongue up against the palate and pulling the chin and abdomen inwards help to close the air-passage and facilitate performance of the Vipareeta svasa. The benefits are similar.

The above three are described together here, to show the similarity and the differences.

SEETHALI PRANAYAMA
As mentioned earlier, Seethali pranayama tends to cool the body and also to lower the blood pressure.

Sit comfortably on the floor or in a chair.
Breathing in is done through the mouth and breathing out is done through the nose, as follows:

Make a tube of the tongue, by folding the tongue, with the tip of the tongue at the lips; and protrude the tube out. Breathe in through the tube of tongue slowly, filling the chest and expanding the chest, filling up the lower lobes of the lungs with air; then pulling the shoulders back, thus filling up the upper lobes of the lungs. Pull the tongue in and close the lips together.

Hold the breath briefly, raising the tongue to the front half of the palate and pulling the abdomen in. Lock the chin to the upper chest (also known as

Jalandhara Bandha or Chin-lock).

Breathe out slowly, relaxing the chest and abdomen.
Repeat three to six times.

UJJAYI PRANAYAMA:

Ujjayi breathing is an important pranayama to learn, as it can often be an integral part of other Yoga practices, such as meditation, mantra yoga, kriya yoga, nadi-sodhana pranayama, surya-namaskaram and during the practice of the yoga asanas described earlier. Ujjayi breathing will enhance the benefit, when combined with such practices.

Ujjayi breathing is similar to the action of smelling a flower, for example.

Sit comfortably and take a deep breath in, with both nostrils; notice the back of the mouth opening up during the slow and deep breathing. Then partially close the back of the throat with the *epiglottis*, similar to the swallowing action, and breathe out with force; notice the 'hissing' or 'snoring' sound the expiration makes.

Raising the tongue up to the palate and pulling the chin and abdomen inwards also help to close the throat partially.

Next try the Ujjayi breathing, during inhalation also, and the same 'hissing' sound can be heard.

Now do the Ujjayi breathing in both inhalation and exhalation, after closing the glottis and trachea with epiglottis, as described above, with same duration for both inhalation and exhalation.

Ujjayi Pranayama with Kumbakha:
After partially closing the glottis with epiglottis, Inhale through both nostrils; retain the breath with Jalandhara bandha or chin-lock, described previously under 'Kumbakha'; release the chin-lock; then exhale through the left nostril, by closing the right nostril with the right thumb.

What is Epiglottis?
Epiglottis is a flap-like cartilage, covered with mucus membrane, and is situated in the pharynx, behind the root of the tongue, above the *larynx.*
In normal breathing, the epiglottis is up and relaxed, allowing the breathing to take place through the trachea.
While swallowing food or liquid, the epiglottis is pushed down by elevation of the neighboring *hyoid bone.* This makes the epiglottis to close the *glottis and trachea,* preventing food or liquid to enter the trachea. It is the epiglottis that is pushed down to partially close the trachea in Ujjayi breathing.

7. ON MEDITATION

Meditation as a discipline is one of the most important aspects of mind management. Very often, people complain that when they sit for meditation other thoughts come and disturb them and their thoughts take them for a ride and for many, it is very difficult to bring the concentration back to meditation especially in the beginning. The reason is, the mind itself consists of a flow of thoughts. It is best to ignore the flow of thoughts. With more practice in meditation, it will become easier to manage such thoughts.

Ardha Padmasana

This is one of the Yoga poses for meditation. However, any comfortable position on the floor or a chair is acceptable.

It is best to do meditation after a brief session of Pranayama; however, one need not become proficient in Pranayama, before starting meditation.

A brief description is given on different meditation methods that can be helpful in keeping the focus on meditation:

1. Meditation based on objects to observe:
Objects to observe can be either a lamp or candle, so that the meditator can focus on the light, to develop *concentration* in the beginning. Here, there is subject-object relationship, until the person can go on to deeper meditation without the help of the objects. Then the subject-object relationship drops off.

2. Meditation based on breathing:
In this method, sit comfortably and merely observe normal breathing, inhalation and exhalation. With practice, this observation will bring your mind to a calm status, where you can stay and continue meditation. As the observation or awareness of breathing continues, the breathing slows, leading to deeper meditation, where Awareness alone remains.

3. Meditation based on a Mantra word: Mantra

yoga:

When a word or sentence– for example, OM (AUM)– is repeated mentally, the mind becomes calmer. When the same Mantra is repeated several times, there is 'silence' between the Mantra. The silence that lies between the Mantra word or words, becomes longer and longer, and eventually makes the mind abide in the 'silence'. The word silence is used here for lack of a better word to denote the Changeless Truth which is the ultimate goal of meditation. In fact, all yoga systems are formulated to lead towards this ultimate goal.

4. Meditation based on *Nadis and Chakras*:
Kundalini yoga:

Nadis are *subtle* nerve-like structures and they are distributed all over the body. Different ancient Yoga texts state different numbers for the total number of nadis to be over 300,000; however, it is generally considered to be a total of 72,000 nadis. Pranic or life-energy flows through them. When the flow is blocked, Life energy or Pranic energy cannot adequately flow through the nadis, giving rise to diseases and disturbance in the normal internal environment.

There are three main nadis along the spine; they are *Sushumna nadi, Ida nadi and Pingala nadi.* Sushumna Nadi is the most important and runs in the middle of the spinal column from the base of the spine to the top of the head. The Energy-Conciousness or the

Pranic Energy that is concentrated in the lowest part of Sushumns nadi is called the *Kundalini Sakti* and is said to be coiled in three and a half circles like a snake. It is supposed to be lying dormant, until it rises up in the Sushumn nadi in the spine.

The Ida nadi runs to the left of the spinal column and the Pingala nadi runs to the right of the spinal column. They are also subtle energy nadis. Generally speaking, Ida nadi represents the para-sympathetic system and Pingala nadi represents the sympathetic system. They intertwine with each other at different centers and merge with the Sushumna nadi in the *Ajna Chakra,* situated between the eyebrows.

Chakras are *subtle centers of Energy-Consciousness*. They are not anatomical structures but they are similar to the nerve-plexusus of the body distributed along the midline from the base of the spine to the top of the head. They are centers of Life energy or Pranic energy situated in the center of spine. There are mainly seven chakras and there are also other minor chakras. Each chakra has a lotus-like arrangement of petals; and the petals vary in number for each chakra. The number of petals represent the number of subtle nadis, arising from them. Each chakra, except for the *Sahasrara,* represents a *bija mantra (seed mantra).* The lower five Chakras are associated with the five elements of space, air, fir, water and earth.

A brief description of the the seven main chakras are given here as follows:

Mooladhara Chakra is at the lower end of the Sushumna nadi, in the pelvic floor. In women, it is said to be in the uterine cervix. It is associated with the sacral plexus in the human body. It has four petals; mantra is *Lam;* the element is earth.

Swadhistana Chakra is about two inches behind the Mooladhara chakra and is associated with sacral and prostatic plexuses. It has six petals; mantra is *Vam;* the element is water.

Manipura Chakra is in the spinal column, at the level of the navel and is associated with solar plexus. It has ten petals; mantra is *Ram;* the element is fire.

Anahata Chakra is situated close to the heart and associated with cardiac plexus. It has twelve petals; mantra is *Yam;* the element is air.

Vishuddhi Chakra is in the middle of the throat. It is associated with cervical plexus in the neck area. It has sixteen petals; mantra is *Ham; the element is space.*

Ajna Chakra is behind the center of the eyebrows at the top of the spinal column and is a very important landmark in the practice of meditation. It is associated with mind and intelligence and is the ruler of all the lower centers. It has two petals; mantra is *Om*.

Sahasrara Chakra is the seventh and the highest of the major chakras. It is situated in the crown of the head, at the level of the anterior fontanelle. It is associated with the causal body or the *Most Subtle* body.

Among the minor chakras, *Lalana Chakra,* situated in the back of the throat, opposite the epiglottis, is an important chakra. Purification of the Nadis and Chakras, with the practice of different asanas and Pranayama is an important preliminary step for meditation on Chakras as well as for general well-being of the human body.

It is said the microcosm is similar to and the prototype of macrocosm. In that sense, the human body, being the microcosm of the *cosmos,* the lower five chakras up to *Vishuddhi* represent the five elements of space, air, fire, water and earth i.e., the *gross body.*

The *Ajna Chakra* represents the *subtle body* of the microcosm, the human body.
An example of the subtle body of the cosmos, in the present-day knowledge, would be *the Dark Matter and Dark Energy,* the origin and functioning of which are still unclear, and are being extensively investigated by *Physicists.*

The Sahasrara Chakra in this context, would be the *Most Subtle Body* of the *microcosm*, the human body. The *Most Subtle* Body of the *macrocosm* is also called the *Causal body* by *Philosophers*.

The Absolute Changeless Truth, the ultimate goal of all the seekers of wisdom, in this author's opinion, is beyond the gross, subtle and the *Most Subtle* of the *macrocosm as well as the microcosm.*
After gaining knowledge of the Chakras, the meditator is advised to raise Awareness from the lower to the higher chakras one by one, very gradually and ultimately to realize the Changeless Truth. This meditation will require guidance from a teacher who is familiar with the method.

THE ULTIMATE GOAL:

In any of the methods described, when the meditator becomes proficient, he is said to be in deep meditation, leading to the ultimate goal, which is for the mind to abide in Limitless Awareness. The Life Energy, inherent in the Limitless Awareness is the source of all things in the Universe, all the animate and inanimate things in the world as well as the billions and billions of galaxies.

The Life Energy, in the Most Subtle State remains as a potential, inherent in the Limitless Awareness.

When the mind ultimately abides in Limitless Awareness–that being the *Origin of All Things in Nature–* it is called the Savikalpa Samadhi.

When the mind ultimately abides in Limitless Awareness– that being the *Changeless Truth–* it is called the Nirvikalpa Samadhi.

There is no subject-object relationship; there is no meditator, object of meditation and the process of meditation; there is no observer, observed and observation. The meditator is said to be established in "Steady wisdom".

BIBLIOGRAPHY

Akira, Saura and Niwa, Minae et al. "Adolescence Stress Induced Epigenetic Control of Dopaminergic Neurons via Glucocorticoids." Science volume 339. Published January 18, 2013: pages 335-339.

Bhat, Vasanthi. "The Power of Conscious Breathing in Hatha Yoga." Second edition published by Vasanthi Bhat in 2002.

Carney, D. R., A. J. C. Cuddy, and A. J. Yap. "Power Posing: Brief Nonverbal Displays Affect Neuroendocrine Levels and Risk Tolerance." *Psychological Science* 21.10 (2010): 1363-368. Web.

Geuze, et al. "Reduced GABA Benzodiazepine Receptor Binding in Veterans with Post-Traumatic Stress Disorder." Molecular Psychiatry, 2008, pages 74-83.

Iyengar, B. K. S.. "Light on Yoga." Published by Schocken; revised edition (1979).

Kessler, Christian, Et Al. "Yoga for Chronic Neck Pain: A Pilot Randomized Controlled Clinical Trial." *The Journal of Pain* 13.11 (2012): 1122-130. Web.

Kirkwood, et al. "Yoga for Anxiety: A Systematic Review of Research Evidence." British Journal of Sports Medicine, 2005: pages 884-891.

Lidell, Lucy. "The Sivananda Companion to Yoga." Published by Touchstone in 2000.

Muktibodhananda S. *Hatha Yoga Pradapika*. New Delhi: Bihar School of Yoga, 1985. Print.

Sherman Et Al, K. J. "A Randomized Trial Comparing Yoga, Stretching, and a Self-care Book for Chronic Low Back Pain." *Archives of Internal Medicine* 171.22 (2011): 2019-026. Web.

Streeter, Chris C., MD. "Yoga Asana Sessions Increase Brain GABA Levels." *The Journal of Alternative and Complementary Medicine* 13.4 (2007): 419-26. Print.

Torgerson, David J., Et Al. "Yoga: A Cost-Effective Treatment for Back Pain Sufferers?" *Science Daily*. University of York, 16 Aug. 2012. Web. 5 Oct. 2013. <http://www.sciencedaily.com/releases/2012/08/120816075405.htm>.

Tronche, Francois et al. "Chronic Stress Triggers Social Aversion via Glucocorticoid Receptor in Dopaminoceptive Neurons." Science volume 339. Published January 18, 2013: pages 332-335.